Cultural Styles of Knowledge Transmission

CULTURAL STYLES OF KNOWLEDGE TRANSMISSION

Essays in honour of Ad Borsboom

Jean Kommers and Eric Venbrux
(eds)

Routledge
Taylor & Francis Group

LONDON AND NEW YORK

Colofon

First published in 2008 by Amsterdam University Press Ltd.

Published 2025 by Routledge
4 Park Square, Milton Park, Abingdon, Oxon OX14 4RN
605 Third Avenue, New York, NY 10158

Routledge is an imprint of the Taylor & Francis Group, an informa business

ISBN: 9789052602981 (pbk)
ISBN: 9781003693550 (ebk)
DOI: 10.4324/9781003693550

Cover design : Vocking in Vorm, Nieuwegein

For Product Safety Concerns and Information please contact our EU representative:
GPSR@taylorandfrancis.com
Taylor & Francis Verlag GmbH, Kaufingerstraße 24, 80331 München, Germany

Introduction

Jean Kommers and Eric Venbrux

These essays in honour of Ad Borsboom focus on a theme that is central to his long career (from 1972 onwards) in the service of Pacific Studies in the Netherlands, and in particular of Aboriginal Studies: the transmission of knowledge. As a prominent 'life long fieldworker', Ad has always been engaged in this subject, which he approached from different angles. First, like every anthropologist while doing fieldwork, he was interested in learning from his hosts – not merely by acquiring 'data', but first and foremost by 'learning lessons'. These lessons, which left a profound impression on him, confronted him in most fundamental ways with his own, 'western' epistemology and worldview. It motivated Ad later to share his insights and experiences with colleagues and students, and in particular with 'the general public': he became a tireless advocate for the world he had so intimately familiarised himself with: in television and radio broadcasts, in newspapers, for visitors of museums, such as the Aboriginal Art Museum, and in extra-academic courses he tried to transfer his insights. Deserving a special mention is his 'long seller' *De clan van de Wilde Honing* ('The Sugarbag Clan'). He even cooperated in an exhibition project for the Tropical Museum Junior in Amsterdam in 1995. In this award-winning exhibition, *Verhalen om niet te verdwalen* ('Stories so as not to get lost'), at the children's museum, and in the accompanying educational materials, Ad again shared many of the insights he had gained in Arnhem Land, Australia, over the years. What is more, he thoroughly discussed the exhibition with the Djinang – the Aboriginal people he worked with – and commissioned them to create artefacts and art works especially for the event. The successful show included performances and special effects. Moreover, it presented visitors with a view of the present-day way of life of the Djinang, using modern means of communication and transportation. The transfer of knowledge was the underlying concept of the exhibition in more than one way: children (between the ages of six and twelve) were first invited to experience the exhibition on their own. Thereafter, they were given the opportunity to show their parents or caretakers around, thus transmitting to the adults the knowledge they had acquired during their first visit.

In his book *De clan van de Wilde Honing*, Ad faced a double challenge. Firstly, he had to inform a lay public about knowledge systems that are completely alien to the Dutch worldview. Moreover, he aspired to transmit knowledge about the transmission of knowledge. Besides his aim to provide an insight into the ways in which Aborigines conceptualize their physical and spiritual environment, Ad also tried to make it accessible to a general public how Aboriginals customarily educate the younger generations. He wrote about their pedagogical principles, which he personally experienced over a period of several decades.

Therefore, we thought it appropriate to choose as a theme for this collection of essays on the occasion of his retirement *Cultural Styles of Knowledge Transmission*. In the following contributions, the authors pay attention to a wide variety of subjects touching upon this theme. Some articles concentrate on ways in which anthropological field-workers experience their learning of other cultures *in situ*, while others pay special attention to local epistemologies, 'exotic' pedagogical strategies, the anthropologist as a mediator between different knowledge systems, and so on.

In his long career, Ad not only was a gifted fieldworker and an advocate of Aboriginal cultures, his diplomatic and social capabilities, so essential to a fieldworker, also served him in a major management position. In the modern academic world, management takes up a central position and it was in this sphere that Ad during many years contributed to developments in the Faculty of Social Sciences and the Department of Cultural Anthropology. Therefore, this collection starts with a contribution by the former Dean of the Faculty.

We sincerely regret that one contribution is missing in this book. In an early phase, Ad's former teacher and colleague, Professor Albert Trouwborst, promised the editors a contribution about the *umushin-gantahe*, a kind of judge, arbitrator or councillor in Burundi. To attain such a position, a man had to take a particular course of instruction, and had to pass certain tests, providing proof of his abilities. On 17 October 2007, Professor Trouwborst passed away. Shortly before his death, Albert Trouwborst completed a draft of his monograph *Leven op de heuvelen van Burundi* ('Living on the Hills of Burundi'), to which we may refer readers interested in this subject.

Three other mentors of Ad, the late Lex van der Leeden, Kenneth Maddock and Les Hiatt, should also be mentioned. Ad in turn mentored and inspired a great many people, something we in Nijmegen are thankful for. Thanks are due to René van der Haar, the ever-cheerful documentalist of the Centre for Pacific and Asian Studies, for his assistance in compiling this collection, and to Geert Bors for correcting the English language of a number of contributions. And finally, we are grateful for the generous subsidy for the publication of this volume that the Department of Cultural Anthropology at Radboud University Nijmegen provided.

* * *

Ad Borsboom

Charles de Weert

Anthropologists are observers of others and of themselves. The latter is a necessary condition for a healthy dose of self mockery and for a sense of perspective. These two properties are amply available in the person of Ad Borsboom. It would be tempting to present a specimen of his idiosyncratic sense of humour, but I am afraid that his jocular style is too refined to be committed to paper properly. Empathy, a further indispensable quality for a good anthropologist, is another of Ad's prominent attributes. It is only fair to say that this admirable trait must have cost Ad tremendous amounts of time, as, precisely because of his empathic powers, he was an intermediary par excellence. Difficult jobs almost naturally landed on his desk. I will not mention all the affairs he was requested to solve; it suffices to confess that we were clever enough to use (some might say 'abuse') his 'I cannot be blamed for this'-face on a number of occasions. The working title of this Liber Amicorum has been 'Teaching and Learning in Unknown Cultures'. A period of administrative duties as a vice-dean must at least have embodied a bit of 'learning in strange cultures' for Ad, just as my deanship contained a strong component of learning in strange cultures for me.

In my first round of 'functioning discourses' with the faculty's full professors, I tried to unite the members of the societal sciences (Sociology, Anthropology and Developmental Studies, Communication Science) under what I thought was their common denominator: Sociology. Although Ad has always championed his field of cultural anthropology very ardently, I received a fair share of support from him for my endeavour. Unfortunately, my attempts were not very fruitful. It was clear from discussions I had with Ad and with one of his PhD students (who later became an important person at the Faculty Bureau) that, although they could agree with my statement with respect to general theories, they added some important insights: sociologists observe global entities or systems, whereas anthropologists not only observe groups but also the behaviour of individuals, and as such would probably have more in common with psychologists. I also learned more about a quintessential difference between anthropology and other social sciences: while sociologists and to some extent psychologists generally study what people say they do, a basic assumption of anthropologists is that what people say they do, often differs considerably from what they actually do in daily life. Moreover, what people say they do and what they actually do, varies within different contexts and periods of time. That is why protracted fieldwork, including participant observation, forms the most vital research method of anthropologists. After all, Ad has taught me more about anthropology than I could edify him with regards to psychology.

Ad as an Administrator

As a director of the NICI research institute, I was the institute's representative towards the Faculty Board. I am ashamed to say that I hardly remember what occurred at these Board meetings at the beginning, say in 1987, as its structure was completely different for what it is today.

From 1995 onwards, Ad was a member of the Faculty Board. He served as a vice-dean, while Professor Giesbers was the dean, and continued when Professor Gerris took over from Giesbers in 1997. In the period from 2001 to 2003, I became Ad's colleague as a vice-dean under Gerris's deanship. I am still grateful for his period as a vice-dean during the time I was the Faculty dean (2003-2007).

I cannot remember any verbal collisions with Ad. We may possibly have disagreed sometimes on our preferences of the best possible strategy, although I do not even remember such instances. There has not been a single issue, however delicate or knotty, on which we did not arrive at a common viewpoint.

Ad has a set of particular characteristics that make him by far the most suitable person for a good personnel management. Unsurprisingly, Ad presided over a committee on personnel management with great dexterity and an unsurpassed ability to identify himself with people on all levels of the organisation. Add to that his great sense of humour, and one can understand how his face, which regularly radiated that aura of 'You cannot blame me for this', won over even the most unwavering adversary. He really is a captivating person. In his book *The Clan of the Wild Honey*, one can easily distinguish both his humour and his winning ways.

In many instances, Ad indeed was the ideal intermediary – especially when particular differences in scientific practices became apparent between the groups I was familiar with and parts of the faculty, which I still had to get acquainted with. At those moments, it became particularly apparent that Ad and I came from largely different cultures of science, with very diverse research modes. Let me entice you with one brief example: at NICI, the master-apprentice relation was virtually sacred. In my view, it had to be adopted as an ideal model for the interaction between the staff and the PhD students at all sections of our faculty. We at NICI even thought that it should also be applied to the relation between staff and master students. I still like to call it the Coffee Vending Machine Paradigm: very frequent contacts are paramount in this model, be it that these do not always need to be direct – a talk at the coffee machine sometimes suffices. However, I learned that this model simply did not apply to anthropology, due to the specific task of anthropology, i.e. sending out students to study other and mostly distant cultures. It would be tough to meet at a coffee machine halfway. Ad was aware that this tradition has its dangerous sides: students can easily get accustomed to the lures of a free life abroad, but of course they also gain strength in personality. For the faculty, the local (NICI) model was more favourable because of the higher study efficiency. There were many more cultural differences. A substantial difference, often discussed with Ad concerned our section's publication strategies. Anthropologists (Masters and PhD students) write an Opus Magnum; experimental psychologists try to produce papers in journals. Things are rapidly changing nowadays.

Ad as a Colleague

Ad was a vice-dean from 1995 until last year. He is not the kind of person who would ever boast about such a position, although he certainly must have had his share of weighty and roaring events since his start. It is hardly possible to find a better one. When I was to become the dean for a period of four years, my condition towards the

7

University Board was that Ad Borsboom should stay on as a vice-dean, despite the fact that he really had deserved a sabbatical after eight years of vice-deanship. In our team Ad continued his important work as the chairman of the budget distribution committee. In this particular function, his very disarming facial expression helped us through the budget debate in record time. There were only two short meetings required: a preparatory one to set out the basic principles and one to divide the means. Ad prepared these meetings very well.

It is good to remark that in a management team many more subtleties play their parts. To all those subtleties Ad made very valuable contributions.

Ad ended his official career at the same date I did, May 1st, 2007. His natural and familiar links with Australia will certainly keep him and Elfrida strongly connected to this country. I wish both of them a very good time after his retirement.

Contents

Ad in the Outback. Photo J. Altman

Maradjiri and Mamurrng: Ad Borsboom and Me

Jon Altman

My copy of Ad Borsboom's thesis *Maradjiri: A Modern Ritual Complex in Arnhem Land, North Australia* is notated on the imprint first page 'J.C. Altman, Dept of Prehistory + Anthro, The A.N.U., May 1979' so I must have taken this book into the field with me when I travelled to Maningrida in April 1979. Nicolas Peterson, my supervisor, must have given it to me.

It was a year later, in May 1980, when I first met Ad. Actually, it was Elfrida whom I almost met first. I had been living at an outstation called Mumeka with Kuninjku people over the wet seasons, cut off from Maningrida owing to seasonal flooding of the bush track that ran past Mumeka. The contact that Mumeka residents and I had with the outside world was via the Liverpool River and a landing called Manbulkardi about 10 kilometres from the outstation. I had been living at Mumeka since October 1979 and in May travelled to Maningrida by boat for one of my rare visits to the township. I went into the local MPA (shorthand for the Maningrida Progress Association) shop, and there I saw this exquisite Balanda (non-Aboriginal) woman and my mind raced. Unfortunately, I soon found out that she was Mrs Borsboom, living at Maningrida, with two young daughters Jacqueline and Sandra and the anthropologist Dr Ad Borsboom. Despite my initial disappointment, the Borsbooms and I formed a long-standing intercontinental friendship.

Maradjiri was a big part of my early bonding at Maningrida with Jimmy Burinyila, a Djinang man of the Mildjingi clan who had also worked with Borsboom; I was then a young economist metamorphosing into an anthropologist and Burinyila and I used to talk a lot about ceremonial exchange. Burinyila was the son of Raiwalla who had been a close collaborator (we used to call them informants, but they were actually the people who made our cross-cultural engagements possible) of the anthropologist Donald Thomson. Thomson had written an early book *Economic Exchange and the Ceremonial Exchange Cycle in Arnhem Land* that struggled with explaining the hybrid economic and social institution embedded in trade ceremonies. Maradjiri was one of these ceremonies and Borsboom's thesis had investigated how the pre-colonial Maradjiri had transformed in colonial times from a post-burial ceremony to a 'birth pole' ritual that celebrated a child's birth several years after the event. Borsboom differentiated 'old' from 'modern' Maradjiri which was a clever distinguishing device that avoided the inadequate and problematic term 'traditional'.

By the time I met Ad I had become heavily associated with Kuninjku-speaking people (what could perhaps be described, as Borsboom (2005) hints in his recent contribution 'Thomson at Gaartji', as a language 'community'). These people spoke the eastern dialect of Bininj Kunwok ('the people's language') and were often referred to as eastern Kunwinjku. But like Borsboom, my interest in exchange recognised that this language (or dialect) group had links of sociality, ritual and diplomacy with a far wider community. Indeed Kuninjku were well aware of Maradjiri as an exchange ceremony that they received from the east; and they also had a clan-owned exchange ceremony Mamurrng that they 'gave' in all directions, including the east. During my main period in the field, Kuninjku had been involved in both receiving a Maradjiri ceremony and in assisting by performing as supporting dancers at the giving of two Maradjiri at Ji-balbal and Gamardi outstations by a Gunartpa man, Robert Bibora, who was then residing uxorilocally at Mumeka.

Ad and I formed a close personal and professional relationship quickly – so much so that I invited him, or he invited himself with Dutch directness, to come and visit me at Mumeka in June 1980. This is a long time ago, 28 years to be precise, but I found proof of Ad's visit in my photographic archive (see the picture at the start of this essay) when we visited Mimanjar and observed the making of a conical fish trap by the now deceased Anchor Kulunba. I also found reference to Ad to in my field diary entry of 3 June 1980 'an interesting day with Art [sic] Borsboom'. I think Ad was a little intrigued by Kuninjku because they were one of the language communities that were most committed to living at outstations as modern day hunter-gatherers: Ad had observed Kuninjku move to Mumeka when he first did fieldwork in the Maningrida region in 1972 and 1973; they were still there in 1980 (as they are in 2008) while the Djinang group with whom he worked seemed to find it more difficult to maintain viable outstations and lived primarily in Maningrida township.

Ad and my interest in ceremony had very different origins. Ad used the Maradjiri ceremony as his kaleidoscope to observe Djinang cosmology and contemporary (1970s) Djinang ceremonial life: the Maradjiri was a dominant institution of the Wurgigandjar clan with whom he has worked since 1972 and was integral to their identity. My interest in Mamurrng, the corresponding exchange ceremony of the Kuninjku (and especially the Kurulk clan) focused primarily on its role as an economic 'exchange' institution, although by 1979 this role had diminished considerably in significance. Indeed both Maradjiri and Mamurrng had changed considerably by the 1970s.

One transformation was economic. Historically, such ceremonies provided opportunity for exchange of goods in association with a large gathering, as well as payment in goods to the givers of the ceremony. This was Thomson's ceremonial exchange cycle whereby scarce goods from one direction were traded for scarce goods from another direction. By the time that Ad and I did our fieldwork this trade aspect of both ceremonies had been largely usurped by the market that provided commodities. But still these exchange ceremonies persisted as institutions that provided opportunity for social exchange between groups and as a distinct marker of group identity and speciality.

Another transformation was in the focus of the Maradjiri. In his analysis of the ceremony, Borsboom showed how the 'old' Maradjiri has moved from a post-funeral rite to the modern manifestation that celebrates birth. Borsboom (1978) provides a complex analysis of continuity and change in the Maradjiri that I will not elaborate on here except to note that in conclusion he uses an elaborate diagram with a number of directional arrows that shows the radical repositioning of Maradjiri in the human life cycle from a mortuary ritual to a birth celebration ceremony. This leads me to two vignettes, one a little jocular, and the other substantive.

The directional diagram brings to mind a return trip from Darwin that the Borsboom family and I made in June 1980. It is difficult to describe just how hazardous this overland trip of 500 kilometres was then, especially the second half through western Arnhem Land on a seasonal single-vehicle width formed track that wound through the tropical savanna bush. The trip required (and still does) the use of four wheel drive vehicles and often in the early dry season one could become quite disoriented driving through tall vehicle-height spear grass that was yet to be burnt off. As I had driven this track on several occasions in 1979 and 1980, it was my role to show Ad the way from Darwin to Maningrida, but en route we became separated. Between Marrkolidjban and Mumeka outstations I saw Ad's vehicle approaching from the opposite direction through the tall grass. As we pulled alongside on the narrow bush track, Ad put his head out of his truck's window and inquired, in all seriousness, 'why are you driving back to Darwin?' It was late in the afternoon and pointing to the setting sun, I informed Ad that it was he, not I that was driving in a westerly direction. Ad's diagram with its directional arrows reminded me that it is easy to get disoriented in Arnhem Land and that directions can be linear and cyclical and ego-centred.

The directional diagram also resonated with a similar change in Mamurrng that I only discovered by chance. Late in 1980, when I was close to completing my major period of fieldwork and was deeply embedded in Kuninjku social life, I was co-opted to be the manager of a Mamurrng ceremony to be presented to Peter Cooke the senior arts adviser at Maningrida Arts and Crafts to celebrate the births of his children Ira and Louise. Peter had lived in Maningrida since 1972 and had a strong relationship with Kuninjku; he planned to relocate to Darwin at the end of 1981. A lock of hair from each of Peter's children was made into a *kunkodjmud* emblem set in beeswax and decorated with lorikeet feathers and presented to Kevin Djimarr the song and 'magic' man for the Mamurrng ceremony with a request that the ceremony would be performed in a proper 'custom way' (traditional) manner. People at Mumeka took this request, co-brokered with Robert Bibora, very seriously and in September 1981 I was summoned from far-away Canberra to assist Mumeka people enact this ceremony.

This was a very interesting and ambiguous intercultural exchange. On September 29, a ceremony camp was set up in Maningrida that resembled one usually set up for a Lorkkun hollow log (burial) ritual. And Kuninjku people set about producing complicated ritual paraphernalia for nearly a week that included a replica human skeleton carved from wood and a burial platform. People had interpreted the request for a 'traditional' Mamurrng as meaning Mamurrng as a burial ceremony. The finale of the ceremony on October 4 re-enacted a mortuary ritual and at its completion an interesting exchange took place. Peter Cooke paid the ceremonial performers with blankets, lengths of cloth, tobacco, knives, machetes, fishing equipment, pots and pans – highly valued market commodities at that time. Mumeka people gave the Cooke family all the ritual paraphernalia: decorated poles, a bundle of carved wooden (replica) bones, the dancers string decorations, the burial platform, and even a bundle of spears that had come from Mulgurram near Ramingining in an earlier Maradjiri ceremony. All this material culture is now stored at the Northern Territory Museum.

There are many possible interpretations for why this Mamurrng was conducted in this way, like much mortuary ritual it combined sadness about Cooke's imminent departure with celebration of the birth of his children and his dedication to Aboriginal people in the Maningrida region and important contributions to cultural matters. In particular, it was Cooke's vision and commitment that had seen the establishment of the Djómi community museum or keeping place in April 1980. At once this unusual occasion when Kuninjku presented a ceremony to a Balanda demonstrated that the transformation that Ad Borsboom had observed in Maradjiri was replicated in Mamurrng, something that till that time was unknown to researchers.

It also demonstrated something that was very prescient in Ad Borsboom's research in the early 1970s. Ritual as a key component of (Djinang) culture will change in a post-colonial context, but such transformation does not make the modern any less Djinang than the old. And the nature of this change will be influenced by exogamous factors associated with the colonial state, as well as by endogamous factors influenced by Djinang agency. This early exposition of the structure: agency framework and his close attention to colonial and post-colonial historical influences that were so fundamental to Ad

Borsboom's deep and insightful analysis of Maradjiri in the 1970s are critically important parts of his contribution to Oceanic anthropology.

REFERENCES

Borsboom, A. 2005. 'Thomson at Gaartji' eds. B. Rigsby and N. Peterson *Donald Thomson: The Man and Scholar* Canberra, Academy of the Social Sciences in Australia: 159-170.

Borsboom, A. 1978. *Maradjiri: A Modern Ritual Complex in Arnhem Land, North Australia* Nijmegen, Katholieke Universiteit Nijmegen, PhD thesis.

Thomson, D. 1949. *Economic Exchange and the Ceremonial Exchange Cycle in Arnhem Land* Melbourne, Macmillan.

Conversations with Mostapha: Learning about Islamic Law in a Bookshop in Rabat[1]

Léon Buskens

Nous avons encore beaucoup à partager.
Mostapha Naji (1951-2000)

On an April evening in 1988 a fellow PhD student from Leiden introduced me to the owner of a small bookshop in a quiet street in the *ville nouvelle* of Rabat. I had been to the bookshop before, but had not managed to make sense of the highly specialized collection of classics of the Islamic *Schrifttum*, impressive editions in many volumes of religious treatises, historical chronicles, and *belles lettres*. At that time, only a young attendant had been present in the shop, who apparently did not want to force his services upon an unknown visitor. My senior colleague maybe sensed how forlorn I felt as an anthropologist waiting for a research permit in the Moroccan capital, desperately trying to find my way and establishing a network of people with whom I could talk. He praised the learnedness of his friend, as well as his honesty. Mostapha Naji, a bearded man in his late thirties and the owner of *Dar al-turath* ('The Heritage House'), received me in a cordial manner and engaged me in a conversation about my research. Upon entering that evening, I witnessed a scene which I later would recognize as typical: the gathering of a small circle of booklovers and scholars chatting in a relaxed way about discoveries, old and new books, sipping their glass of mint tea or coffee with milk, entertained by their good-humoured host. That evening I left the bookshop with some bio-bibliographical studies, which Mostapha had recommended to me as

---

[1] With many thanks to Nico Kaptein for his introduction to Mostapha, and to Harry Stroomer, David Waines, and the editors of the present volume for their comments. I suppose that the pun on the title of Marcel Griaule's famous book, as well as the implicit reference to Kevin Dwyer's *Moroccan Dialogues*, are obvious.

a good introduction to the study of the Islamic tradition of Morocco.

My countryman returned to Leiden a few days later, having collected enough material in the Moroccan libraries to continue his studies at home. I was only at the beginning of my research on Islamic law and family relations and would have to wait for almost half a year to obtain clearance for fieldwork. Gradually I would start going to the bookshop almost every evening after my work in the libraries and at the University of Rabat. Mostapha always made me feel welcome in his circle of visitors. He would offer me a drink and start to talk about his latest readings or whatever other subject was on his mind. Friends would stop by and we would chat about books and research, under the blazing neon light, surrounded by towering bookshelves full of volumes bound in imitation leather and lettered in fake gold leaf. Sometimes Mostapha's children would come all the way from Salé to see their father, or an itinerant musician would drop in and sing a song for a few coppers. The atmosphere was always relaxed, and the inevitable acquisition of books usually came with a fair reduction, as almost all his customers were also 'friends'.

Thus, the bookshop became my home in a big city, where I felt at ease, always sure to find the reliable company of Mostapha and his two faithful shop-assistants Abdelhafed and Si Mohammed. It was a starting point to build a network of acquaintances. But more important, it became the place where Mostapha initiated me into the study of the classical literary tradition of Morocco. The focus of my research was on contemporary Islamic family law as laid down in a modern law code, the *Mudawwana* (cf. Buskens 1999). However, the contents of this law code was very close to the classical stipulations of Islamic law, which had been laid down in learned treatises, the so-called *fiqh* books (cf. Buskens 1993). I had studied one of these texts for a semester with a teacher at Leiden University, but that was just enough to guide my browsing. In Mostapha's shop I was surrounded by hundreds of these books. Sometimes he would take a carton or open the drawer of his desk and show me a real treasure: a manuscript several centuries old of a text that was unknown or considered lost. Mostapha would read parts of the text to me and explain its meanings and oddities. He would comment on the handwriting, the signs used to introduce marginal annotations, even its smell which might indicate its region of origin, adding references to older and recent studies by Middle Eastern erudites and Western 'orientalists'.

During the months that followed I gradually realized Mostapha's great love of books, and even more of learning from all parts of the world. He showed me rare editions, such as the lithographs that were published in Morocco between circa 1860 and 1940, or the famous Bulaq imprints from nineteenth century Cairo. Thanks to him I managed to compile a collection of the most important works of the Maliki school of Islamic law, which formed the foundation of the Moroccan family code, and without which the law was difficult to understand. Later I realized that Mostapha taught me a crash course in the bibliography of Islamic law. In the nineteenth century the founding fathers of the study of Islamic law in Western academia had great difficulty in identifying the most important legal texts, acquiring copies of these, and understanding them. When I started my studies Dutch scholarship of *fiqh* was on the wane, with the recent retirement of Professor Jan Brugman from Leiden University. But I was so fortunate to find a friendly teacher in a bookshop in Rabat, who was not annoyed about my ignorance, but enjoyed helping me to find my way.

In many ways Mostapha was an ideal *passeur*, being an intermediary between the learned Moroccan tradition of Islamic scholarship, and a naive Dutch anthropologist with a love of book culture. With my feeble knowledge of Islam and Arabic, and the fact that I was not a Muslim, I would hardly have been acceptable as a student to a real Islamic scholar.[2] After finishing secondary school Mostapha had taken some technical training, in which he showed no interest. He lacked any formal schooling in the Islamic sciences, nor did he come from a family of scholars. His father had been a businessman owning a rather prosperous workshop for shutters. His grandfather was a landowner and farmer in the Chaouia, the countryside near Casablanca, about which he always talked with great fondness. Mostapha had acquired his knowledge of the Islamic tradition by extensive reading and by talking with Moroccan and foreign scholars. By chance he had discov-

---

[2] Dale Eickelman has described his relationship as an anthropologist-cum-arabist with a learned judge in Boujad, educated as a traditional scholar, in a famous monograph, which also offers an analysis of the changes in the educational system and in ideas about knowledge in twentieth-century Morocco (Eickelman 1985).

ered that he could make some money by buying and selling old books. At first a travelling middleman, he had set up a shop in mainly new books with the help of a business partner with some money. The bookshop assured him of a constant stream of new books of all sorts, of which he could dispose if he had satisfied his appetite. *Dar al-turath* was also a place where he could meet clients for his real passion, the dealing in old Arabic books and manuscripts. His interest in the contents of books went so far as that he was reluctant to sell books which he considered worthless. He could get upset with me if I nevertheless chose to acquire a book which did not meet his standards.

There also was a normative side to his studies of the classical Islamic tradition. He was a devout believer, combining his interest in *fiqh* with the contemplation of mystical treatises, such as of Ibn `Arabi and of traditional Moroccan authors. His piety went together with a love of life, of beauty, food, music, birds, curious stones and shells, and fishing. He thoroughly enjoyed the poetry of the pre-Islamic era, and jokingly decided that my name in Arabic should be Zuhayr, after one of the great poets of the *Jahiliyya*. Because of his sleuthing and his wide reading he was held in high esteem by many Moroccan scholars, who came to his bookshop to share his discoveries of rare texts, which they would use for their learned publications. The dean of the Moroccan historians, Muhammad al-Mannuni, would sometimes honour *Dar at-turath* with a visit, despite his fragility. Mostapha always received him with great reverence and would ask for his opinion about recent discoveries. Al-Mannuni was the teacher of a generation of nationalist Moroccan historians, and the editor of important collections of historical sources, and at the same time a respected Islamic scholar, having been trained in the traditional Islamic educational system. To express his esteem for Mostapha as a lover of the *turath*, Al-Mannuni gave him a written authorization (*ijaza*) to hand down Islamic knowledge himself, thereby integrating Mostapha in the chain of transmitters of the tradition. Mostapha would transmit his knowledge orally through his generous sharing of information, and by writing down extensive notes in his notebooks (*knanesh* in Moroccan Arabic), in learned letters to his friends, and in his scholarly editions of rare texts, notably in the field of the Islamic law of evidence, the *kutub al-watha'iq*. He also invited other scholars to edit texts which he had discovered and which he considered worthy of publication, investing his own money in these ventures.[3]

Mostapha's curiosity covered many areas beyond the Islamic tradition. The first present, in a long serious of gifts, which he offered me was an Arabic translation of classical Chinese poetry. The experience gained while having been on the road in Europe for several years contributed to Mostapha's skills in imparting his knowledge to foreign researchers. With Joan Baez' songs in the background, Mostapha would relish telling about his life as a hippie in Spain, France, and Switzerland. In his view, his travels in Europe and the Middle East, sharing many pleasures with young people form different cultural backgrounds, had contributed to his becoming a pious man. He combined his deep faith as a Muslim with an intellectual cosmopolitanism which entailed the reading of the mystical treatises of Meister Eckhart and the writing of poems in what he imagined to be a Japanese style. He was always enthusiastic to receive Japanese visitors, some of whom would stay at his house, and we often talked about travelling to Indonesia together, to look at books, food, and people there. His openness was rooted in his upbringing in Casablanca, in Derb Carlotti, whose inhabitants are famous for their relaxed and liberal attitude. Communication with foreigners was further helped by Mostapha's command of the French language. If necessary, he would also make an attempt to speak English or Spanish. He was always eager to talk with people in order to acquire new ideas and impressions. He enjoyed sharing his knowledge and ideas, hoping for a real exchange. Above anything else, being with him was a pleasure because of his sense of humour, his honesty, and his profound humanity.[4]

---

[3] A bibliography of Mostapha Naji's publications will be part of a planned memoir of my lamented friend. One provisional result of his teachings in this field, with references to some of these editions, is my 1995 article, which Mostapha considered not sufficiently focused on the ancient sources.

[4] Unfortunately, the format of this short contribution does not allow for a systematic analysis of the exchange of friendship, knowledge, books, presents, and money, in which Mostapha and I were involved. Several anthropologists have written about these aspects of fieldwork in Morocco, most notably Rabinow (1977). Driessen (1984) presents an overview and critical appraisal of some of these 'experimental' contributions. The sympathetic collection of portraits of individual as exercises in social history edited by Burke (1993) offers a valuable framework for further analysis.

At the end of my first stay in Rabat, Mostapha had initiated me in the book culture of classical Islamic scholarship in the Maghreb, which would be the foundation of many of my publications. A few weeks before leaving for the Netherlands, Mostapha showed me the extent to which he had come to trust me by inviting me to join him on a trip to Meknes and Fez in order to look for manuscripts for his business. It would be the first of many travels in Morocco which would entail for me a further initiation in the book trade, as well as in Moroccan culture. It was the next step in a friendship which came to a sad end with 'my elder brother's' untimely death in September 2000.

REFERENCES

Burke III, E. ed. 1993. *Struggle and Survival in the Modern Middle East* London, I.B. Tauris.

Buskens, L. 1993. 'Islamic Commentaries and French Codes: The Confrontation and Accomodation of Two Forms of Textualization of Family Law in Morocco' ed. H. Driessen *The Politics of Ethnographic Reading and Writing: Confrontations of Western and Indigenous Views* Saarbrücken, Breitenbach Publishers: 65-100.

Buskens, L. 1995. 'Maliki Formularies and Legal Documents: Changes in the Manuscript Culture of the `Udul (Professional Witnesses) in Morocco' ed. Y. Dutton *The Codicology of Islamic Manuscripts: Proceedings of the Second Conference of Al-Furqan Islamic Heritage Foundation 4-5 December 1993* London, Al-Furqan Islamic Heritage Foundation: 137-145

Buskens, L. 1999. *Islamitisch recht en familiebetrekkingen in Marokko* Amsterdam, Bulaaq.

Driessen, H. 1984. *Konfrontatie, bekentenis en betekenis: Over experimentele etnografie* Nijmegen, Vakgroep Culturele Antropologie, Katholieke Universiteit Nijmegen, Publicatie Serie No. 14.

Eickelman, D.F. 1985. *Knowledge and Power in Morocco: The Education of a Twentieth-Century Notable* Princeton, Princeton University Press.

Rabinow, P. 1977. *Reflections on Fieldwork in Morocco* Berkeley, University of California Press.

Education in Eighteenth Century Polynesia

Henri J.M. Claessen

Because of the limited size allowed for an article in this *Festschrift*, this can be no more than a short reconnaissance of the educational field, concentrating on Polynesia in the second half of the eighteenth century, when European visitors arrived at the islands. I will use here mainly the observations of eighteenth century Europeans, though their observations on education are merely incidental in nature, and scattered in bits and pieces over their journals. This is not surprising, for education in the islands was rather informal and hardly structured.

Generally speaking, education was received at home. The boys imitated their fathers (uncles, elder brothers), the girls assisted their mothers (sisters, aunts) and thus learned the household chores. One of the few visitors who made some coherent observations on the education of Polynesian boys and girls was the naturalist-philosopher Johann Reinhold Forster, who accompanied James Cook on his second voyage (1772-1775). His description, summarizing his observations of the Tahitian and Tongan situation, is couched in detailed, long winding prose, but therefore has the advantage of being rather comprehensive:

The first notions necessary for the way of life now in use in these islands, are instilled into the tender minds of the children by their parents: these notions may be divided into various branches, as varied as the objects are to which they relate; the more universally necessary objects of all nations, are food, raiment, and shelter against the inclemencies of the weather; the operations therefore relative to food, dress and habitation are the first, which are taught the children by their parents. As these nations [the Polynesian, C.] have not yet a multiplicity of artificial wants, and as their time is not yet taken up with any business more material than the three enumerated articles, their manufactures are in consequence very simple, and undivided in many branches; nay they are all thought necessary for every individual in these isles, and for that reason every child is instructed in the best methods of cultivating the bread-fruit tree, the plantane-stalks, the roots of yams, and other eatable roots; the most expeditious ways for catching fish, the proper season and bait for each kind, and the places which they haunt and resort to, are told to their children; nay all the fishes, shells, and blubbers, which in any ways may with safety be eaten, are named and showed to them, together with their nature, food, haunts, and qualities; the devices for catching birds, for rearing dogs, swine, and fowls, and all the names of spontaneous eatable plants are communicated to their youths, together with their seasons and qualities; so that there is hardly a boy of 10 to 12 years old, who is not perfectly well acquainted with these articles. But as the bark of the mulberry tree, requisite for raiment, must be culti-vated with a great deal of care and application, their youths are well instructed in the methods necessary for that purpose: and every young woman is early instructed in all the operations requi-site for manufacturing and dying their cloth, and likewise in those of making mats, and other parts of their dress. The wood which is best calculated for building a house, a canoe, or other utensils, together with every operation for erecting a habitation, for making the various parts of a boat, and for navigating it by paddles or sails, are understood by every person, from the last *toutou* [servant, C] to the first chief of the land. In short, there is not one mechanical operation, which they do not teach to every youth, and which, after some time, he is not capable of executing with as much adroitness and skill as the best and oldest man in the nation (Forster 1996 [1778]: 270).

Forster gives a rather complete inventory of all that the average boy or girl was taught by their parents and other family members. Yet, some elements of their education are not mentioned. First, there is no indication of instruction in the social and religious notions of their society. And, in view of the complex hierarchical socio-political structure, and the omnipresence of chiefs, gods, ghosts, forefathers, *tapu's*, priests, offerings and *marae*, every boy or girl must have had at least some general knowledge of these topics. Not that Forster was unaware of the importance of social and religious phenomena in Polynesia, but he did not include them in his overview of education. Second, another aspect missing in his summary of the education of the young is sex. This may be explained in view of Forster's rather negative estimations of Polynesian women (Guest 1996).[5]

Considering the great role of sex in traditional Polynesian society, some additional words on the subject are called for. Several authors have discussed the phenomenon in general terms (Sahlins 1985; Claessen 1997). The first visitors of Tahiti already gave ample attention to the 'merry maidens', who visited their ships in considerable numbers, and were willing to exchange sex for all kinds of European goods, preferably nails (Robertson 1955 [1768]: 78). It should be noted, however, that one of the crew members of the Dolphin, Wilkinson (quoted in Warner 1955: 44), stated that several of the girls were 'Directed by the Men to stand in the Prow of their Canoes and Expose their Bodies Naked to Our View'. This indicates some coercion by the men who wanted nails – but on the other hand, 'sex was permitted, encouraged, and considered great fun in Tahiti' (Claessen 1997: 187). The experiences of the crew of the Dolphin were not different from those of the French sailors of De Bougainville, who anchored at Tahiti some months later. The journal of De Bougainville (1966 [1771]), and the writings of his staff members are overflowing with enthusiasm for the more than warm welcome prepared by the 'merry maidens'. Parents invited sailors at home, fed them lavishly, and offered them girls for a kind of public love making, accompanied by songs and music (De Bougainville 1966: 194-195; id. 216). It seems probable that such astounding forms of sexual intercourse were a consequence of the thoroughgoing sexual education of the young. A confirmation of this view can be found in Cook's journal of his first visit of Tahiti (Cook 1968 [1771]: 93-94). In it, Cook describes a scene, in which a very young girl and a boy are having sex in public, surrounded by a number of adults, who, 'far from showing the least disapprobation', instructed the girl 'how she should act her part'. This was certainly a

---

[5] Guest bases her assessment a.o. on the text of Forster's journals.

form of education! Similar observations can be found in the journal of Joseph Banks, who accompanied Cook on this voyage (Banks 1962 [1771] I: 254, 255, 300; II: 330-334). Banks's views can be summarized as: 'Love is the Chief Occupation' on these islands. Even the habitually rather reserved Daniel Solander, the botanist, expresses warm feelings with regard to the Tahitian girls in his journal (Solander 1773: 61, 70). From the observations of the European visitors, it is clear that Tahitian adults provided their children with an – at least in our eyes – very liberal and thorough sexual education.

On other Polynesian islands sexual education and sexual activities were also found to play a profound role in the children's upbringing. For the Hawai'i Islands Sahlins presents the following description:

> Children, at least of the elite, were socialized in the arts of love. Girls were taught the *'amo 'amo*, the 'wink wink' of the vulva, and the other techniques that make 'the tights rejoice'. Young chiefs were sexually initiated by older women, preparing them thus for the sexual conquests that singularly mark a political career; the capture of a senior ancestry. And, all this, of course, was celebrated not only in the flesh, but in dance, poetry, and song (Sahlins 1985: 10).

The whole first chapter of Sahlin's book (1985) is devoted to sex and love; sex, as he presents it, determined the social infrastructure; power could be gained and lost by sexual activities. It is however possible that Sahlins overstated his case somewhat.

Although with local variations, on all other Polynesian islands sex was found to play an crucial role in social life – and thus probably also in education. There are enough data on the sexual situation in, for example, Tonga, and the Marquesas Islands[6] to conclude that children on these isles were likewise thoroughly educated in sexual behaviour so that they, when a little older, would be accomplished performers.

---

[6] For Tonga: G. Forster 1983 [1778]: 400; Gaily 1987: 126-127. On the Marquesas Islands: Marchand, cited in Danielsson 1960: 30; G. Forster 1983 [1778]: 533; Suggs 1963: 119-123.

There were, however, on the islands also specialists, whose education could not be covered by home instruction by relatives. This holds true, for example, for the priests and the navigators. For the additional education in these fields, a more formal learning and instruction was required. Priests had to be knowledgeable in their religion, in the world of gods, ghosts and forefathers, in the rites and songs, and in the art of offering (for a surveys of tasks and obligations of priests: Claessen 1995; Henry 1951; Douaire-Marsaudon 1998). Priests (and also priestesses) received a thorough schooling. Oliver (1974: 864-865) mentions the *orometua* as the specialised teachers for Tahiti. This is a general term for instructor. Some of them instructed priests, and taught them the traditions, songs, genealogies and mythology. According to Henry (1951: 81, 86, 91), there were several schools in Tahiti, in which savants of great knowledge were the teachers. Other *orometua* were experts of song and dance and instructed men and women in these arts; the dances, observed by Cook and his companions on Tahiti, Tonga, and Hawai'i were not just improvised movements, but carefully rehearsed songs and ballets [7]

Navigators comprise another group of specialists. This category does not refer to men who, on occasion, could steer their canoe from Tahiti to Moorea, or were equipped to undertake comparable short voyages, but rather to the men specialised in long-distance sailing. These navigators could find their way on long voyages, using the stars, the moon, the waves, and other signs that could be observed on their seafaring journeys.

Most data on these navigators have been collected long after the traditional art of sailing had died out, and was replaced by European ships and techniques. It is mainly thanks to the detailed studies by David Lewis (1972), and Geoffrey Irwin (1992) that we now know how traditional navigators determined their course, on the basis of continually changing patterns of stars. Our knowledge has improved greatly in the last years, for only in 1962 (Golson, ed. 1962) we hardly knew how such voyages were made, and whether they were of a deliberate or accidental nature. The education of the navigators was long

---

[7] On Hawaii: Cook 1967 [1778]: 284, 285. On Tahiti: Cook 1969 [1775]: 208, 209. On Tonga: Cook 1969 [1775]: 246, 272-273.

and thorough. They had to learn the various patterns of stars and the seasonal influences by heart ; they had to have a sound knowledge of Oceanic topography, and their only 'maps' were schematic constructions of branches and shells. And yet, they succeeded in taking their ships to their intended destinations – though sometimes it took quite a long time, as becomes apparent in Mariner's descriptions of the unfortunate voyage of the Tongan chief (1819: 276-285).

REFERENCES

Banks, J. 1962 [1771]. *The Endeavour Journal of Joseph Banks* ed. J.C. Beaglehole Sydney, Angus and Robertson, 2 vols.

Bougainville, L.-A. de 1966 [1771]. *Voyage autour du monde* ed. M. Hérubel Paris, Union Générale d'Editions, Le Monde en 10/18.

Claessen, H.J.M. 1995. 'The Oro-Maro-Arioi Connection' eds. D.A.M. Smidt, P.ter Keurs and A.Trouwborst *Pacific Material Culture* Leiden, Rijksmuseum voor Volkenkunde, Mededelingen van het Rijksmuseum voor Volkenkunde No. 28: 282-292.

Claessen, H.J.M. 1997. 'The Merry Maidens of Matavai' *Bijdragen tot de Taal-, Landen Volkenkunde* 152:183-210.

Cook, J. 1967 [1778]. 'Journal' ed. J.C. Beaglehole *The Journals of Captain James Cook: The Voyage of the Resolution and Discovery, 1776-1780* Cambridge, Cambridge University Press, Hakluyt Society Extra Series No. 36: 1-491.

Cook, J. 1968 [1771]. 'Remarkable Occurrences on Board His Majesty's Bark Endeavour' ed. J.C. Beaglehole *The Journals of Captain James Cook: The Voyage of the Endeavour, 1768-1771* Cambridge, Cambridge University Press, Hakluyt Society Extra Series No. 34: 1-479.

Cook, J. 1969 [1775]. 'Journals on Board His Majesty's Bark Resolution' ed. J.C. Beaglehole *The Journals of Captain James Cook: The Voyage of the Resolution and Adventure, 1772-1775* Cambridge: Cambridge University Press, Hakluyt Society Extra Series No. 35: 1-628.

Danielsson, B. 1960. *Forgotten Islands of the South Sea* London, Harborough.

Douaire-Marsaudon, F. 1998. *Les premiers fruits: Parenté, identité sexuelle et pouvoirs en Polynésie occidentale (Tonga, Wallis et Futuna)* Paris, Éditions de la Maison des Sciences de l'Homme, Chemins de l'Ethnologie.

Forster, G. 1983 [1778]. *Reise um die Welt* ed. G. Steiner Frankfurt am Main, Insel.

Forster, J.R. 1996 [1778]. *Observations Made during a Voyage round the World* ed. N. Thomas, H. Guest and M. Dettelbach Honolulu, University of Hawai'i Press.

Gailey, C.W. 1987. *Kinship to Kingship: Gender, Hierarchy and State Formation in the Tongan Islands* Austin: University of Texas Press.

Golson, J. ed. 1962. *Polynesian Navigation: A Symposium on Andrew Sharp's Theory of Accidental Voyages* Wellington, Polynesian Society, Memoir No. 34.

Guest, H. 1996. 'Looking at Women: Forster's Observations in the South Pacific' eds. N. Thomas, H. Guest and M. Dettelbach *Observations Made during a Voyage round the World, by J.R. Forster* Honolulu, University of Hawai'i Press: xli-lv.
Henry, T. 1951 [1928]. *Tahiti aux temps anciens* translated by B. Jaunez Paris, Musée de l'Homme, Publications de la Société des Océanistes No. 1.
Irwin, G. 1992. *The Prehistoric Exploration and Colonization of the Pacific* Cambridge, Cambridge University Press.
Lewis, D. 1972. *We, the Navigators: The Ancient Art of Landfinding in the Pacific* Canberra: Australian National University Press.
Mariner, W. 1819. *Nachrichten über die Freundschaflichen, oder die Tonga-Inseln* ed. J. Martin Weimar, Landes Industrie Comptoirs, Neue Bibliothek der Wichtigsten Reisebeschreibungen No. 20.
Oliver, D. 1974. *Ancient Tahitian Society* Honolulu, University of Hawai'i Press, 3 vols.
Robertson, G. 1955 [1768]. *An Account of the Discovery of Tahiti from the Journal of George Robertson, Master of H.M.S. Dolphin* ed. O. Warner London, Folio Society.
Sahlins, M.D. 1985. *Islands of History* Chicago, University of Chicago Press.
Solander, D. 1773. *Journal d'un voyage autour du monde, en 1768, 1769, 1770, 1771, contenant les divers événemens du voyage* Paris, Saillant et Nyon.
Suggs, R.C. 1963. *The Hidden Worlds of Polynesia: The Chronicle of an Archaeological Expedition to Nuku Hiva in the Marquesas Islands* London, Cresset
Warner, O. ed. 1955. *An Account of the Discovery of Tahiti, from the Journal of George Robertson, Master of the Dolphin* London, Folio Society.

From Knowledge
to Consciousness:
Teachers, Teachings, and the
Transmission of Healing

Ien Courtens

'Anthropology is not for whimpers!' was the opening line of Ad Bors-boom's heart-warming laudation at my PhD ceremony. With these words Ad transmitted his final teachings to me and referred to my anthropological fieldwork in the interior of the Bird's Head of West Papua. For 13 months, I lived in the village of Ayawasi to conduct research on healing knowledge and rituals in the context of religious change. It was Ad who taught me the love for the Pacific region through his vivid lectures and made me want to conduct my field research in a Pacific culture. Back at the university again, it was Ad who created the possibility for me to turn my data into a doctoral thesis: his confidence in me and my research made him persistent in finding funds for a PhD position. With commitment and enthusiasm he guided me towards the completion of my thesis.

In Papua, I found a teacher in the person of Maria Baru, one of the most renowned healers in the region of Ayawasi. With wisdom and guidance, she took me under her wing as her student and initiated me into healing knowledge and secrets. She was dedicated to her task of giving me a 'full understanding' of former and contemporary healing performances and knowledge, in the realm of both indige-nous and Christian healing. My journey through the world of healing exposed a rich variety of healing rituals and knowledge. I was taught that the transmission of healing knowledge occurred through initia-tion, dreaming, and a state equal to meditation, by which ancestors reveal messages and ways to heal by transmitting healing methods and secret formulas. Through initiation, dreaming and meditation the essence of their culture is revealed and transferred. These teach-

Freshing up during
fenia meroh.
Photo I. Courtens

ings behold healing in such a way that it brings and restores balances in peoples lives, both physical as well as spiritual. Within the process of religious change, local people searched for ways to restore and maintain balances in their lives, in which the teachings evolved from knowledge to consciousness.

Transmitting Indigenous Healing Knowledge

Let me take you on a short voyage through the teachings of Maria Baru in relation to some elementary parts of the process I referred to above. As a girl, Maria Baru had completed her education as a healer during female initiation, *feniah meroh*. As usual, only the brightest novices received the full training including the most secret healing knowledge. Initiation was a painful, expensive and hard working event. Excluded from communal life the girls stayed a year in the cult house. From sunrise to sunset they were instructed about ancestral regulations and had to memorise the therapeutic effects of 60 to 70 healing plants and accompanying formulas.

As the majority of the population became practising Catholics following the missionaries, people increasingly relied on biomedical treatment of the missionary hospital, which they experience as an 'easy way' of getting cured as it works relatively quickly. Conversely indigenous methods are seen as 'hard work' as you have to search for medicinal leaves, roots and tree bark in the forest. Furthermore, the preparation and use of the ingredients as well as their uptake in the body is time-consuming.

Over the years, initiation rituals disappeared in most Christianized communities. Local people themselves abandoned the rituals because, at that time, this offered them benefits. They regarded 'following modernity', as attractive as it included schooling, Western-style goods and medicine. Within the abolishment-process Maria Baru too, temporarily abandoned her indigenous healing knowledge (see also Louise Thoonen's essay in this volume).

Some decades after initiation rituals were banned, however, people started to revalue the importance of the transfer of certain healing knowledge and practices, a possibility that was lost with the abolishment of the rites. This new awareness led to the reinstatement of a female initiation rite in Maria Baru's native village. Together with five novices I stayed in the cult house. We listened to the ancestral lessons that were transmitted all they long. And just like Maria Baru used to take me into the forest, the novices gathered plants while Maria taught their healing qualities, the accompanying formulas and rituals. The girls cut medicinal leaves, chopped off tree-bark and loped off roots. Back in the cult house, Maria revealed the sacred healing formulas over and over again, until they had internalised the knowledge completely. I learned that healing was enclosed in the repetition of the words and teachings. The repetition made the girls absorb the words until they fully understood and evolved consciousness about the teachings. This is essential because when consciousness evolves, teachings are embodied and mastered, and people can act on them.

Evolving Consciousness on Healing Knowledge

On another level, the feature of evolving consciousness within the process of religious change, a specific group of healers became inspired to create an interesting new form of healing, in which both indigenous and Christian notions and practices are crucial. At the heart of the performances they merge indigenous practices, like dreaming or the application of medicinal leaves and tree-bark, with Christian prayers and symbols, such as the crucifix, a statuette of the Virgin Mary, a rosary, and consecrated water and oil. By combining indigenous and Christian elements, these healers succeeded in incorporating indigenous ways of healing into the biomedical, missionary environment, as they fitted within the missionary context through their Christian character.

Maria Baru is the founder and leader of this new secret society, called *Kelompok Sabda*, the group of God's word. Through visions in meditation, Maria Baru received divine messages in which the necessity of (re-)applying ancestral healing knowledge of the abandoned female initiation rite was emphasised and, simultaneously, (new) knowledge about 'Christian' healing methods was disclosed. The visions not only served as markers for the creation of new healing rituals but, more importantly, as justification for the continuation of certain aspects of indigenous healing performances within a Christian context.

During the healing sessions Maria Baru uses the ancestral formulas she had learned during *fenia meroh* as well as Christian secret formulas and prayers, obtained through the visions. The Christian symbols are employed according to indigenous notions and practices. Healers can 'close the door' of the body of a sick person by making the sign of the cross, with their thumb on top of the head, so that the life breath stays in the body. When a person dies the life breath leaves the body through the head. The consecrated oil or water, a symbol of Christian origin, is applied in the way healers use medical leaves during indigenous healing rites: they rub the fluid on particular parts of the body.

The foundation of the *Kelompok Sabda* was closely linked to the awareness that the religious knowledge missionaries referred to as 'Christian', already existed before the entry of the Church. As the indigenous priest Father Yonatan Fatem stated:

> Our people said prayers long before the Catholic Church entered the area. We have always prayed like we nowadays do in church. Only the words were different. We know about praying in our adat ['tradition']. Yet, in the adat we don't name it praying but reciting a formula (Courtens 2005: 201).

Maria Baru underlined:

> [...] we already knew the Bible [...] When the Catholic Church arrived, they just used a different naming for what we call *Wefo*. The Bible is similar to *Wefo*. Just like God and Jesus, whom we have always known as *Siway*, the older brother of *Mafif*, the two main characters in our most significant myth: the story of the Creation.
>
> The sign of the cross we recognized as the four directions of the wind [...] Through initiation, the novices learned to work in the four wind directions when performing a major indigenous healing rite. They were taught to walk from head to foot and from left to right alongside the patient when administering certain healing leaves or recite the secret formulas. Thus, the sign of the cross too was already part of our adat (Courtens 2005: 201-2).

Through the *Kelompok Sabda*, people restored the ritual transfer of sacred and secret ancestral healing knowledge, which had stagnated after the abolishment of indigenous initiation rites within the missionary process. *Kelompok Sabda* healers created innovative spiritual healing performances in accordance with 'ways of the Church', but the manner in which the Christian symbols were employed was consistent with ancestral ways as learned during initiation. Thus, with the creation of the *Kelompok Sabda*, a new secret society arose that fitted within the Christian context and in which not only indigenous healing performances but also ancestral notions and practices regarding healing continued in a new form, combined with Christian symbols and practices. Through this awareness people found healing by restoring a balance that was disturbed with the abolition of initiation rites.

Bridging Knowledge and Consciousness

After the completion of my PhD thesis, I searched for ways to converge the knowledge I had attained in Papua, beyond the academic world. Repeatedly Maria Baru had referred to the powers and strength that were given to me and the consequent responsibilities in life. How could I bridge the Papuan world with the academic world? How could I intertwine this new awareness in my life? In the process of searching for answers I found a new teacher in the Netherlands, Loucas van den Berg, MA, spiritual therapist and researcher on the development of new holistic sciences. He guided me into a new way of life and work at the Academy of Music, Education and Healing (in Dutch: AMEG), where people are encouraged to explore and use their total potential of manifestation power, on behalf of their souls. I am admitted into this new scientific world in which I bridge my anthropological knowledge on healing and my academic skills with this new science of the soul and the power of manifestation. In this setting I expand my knowledge and consciousness on healing and my academic work in a spiritual way, based on inner research and the gathering of experience data. In this way, I continue my journey, studying people in all aspects of life. New healing methods are passed on, similar essences discovered, in the awareness that the teaching on and transmission of healing travels from knowledge to consciousness.

REFERENCES

Courtens, I. 2005. *Restoring the Balance: Performing Healing in West Papua* Nijmegen, Radboud University, PhD thesis.
Thoonen, L. 2005. *The Door to Heaven: Female Initiation, Christianity and Identity in West Papua* Nijmegen, Radboud University, PhD thesis.

When 'Natives' Use What Anthropologists Wrote: The Case of Dutch Rif Berbers

Henk Driessen

Since the 1980s, the reflective turn in anthropology has drawn systematic attention to the close link between ethnographic knowledge and power. One important aspect of this connection is the use of ethnographic texts in the politics of identification (cf. Brettell 1993). The rapid advance of digital communication has greatly facilitated the access to, diffusion, transmission and consumption of ethnography, more recently also by what used to be called 'natives' and their offspring.

This essay offers some thoughts on the problems of ethnography consumption outside academia. The recent translation into Dutch of the first part of a standard anthropological monograph on a tribal group in the central Rif (Morocco) and the use of this book by descendants of the original informants in the politics of ethnic identity formation in the Netherlands will be a case in point.

The Politics of Ethnography

Following the publication of *Writing Culture* (1986) and *Anthropology as Cultural Critique* (1986) anthropology went through a period of heightened concern with reflexivity. This trend produced new forms of ethnographic writing, a blurring of genres and the dissemination of a 'new' relativism (Driessen 1993). Some of the changes in the politics of ethnography have partly been imported into the anthropology of the third millennium, although in the last decade we have also seen a partial restoration of ethnographic realism and a silent eclipse of post-modernism (Gingrich and Fox 2002).

More anthropologists began to take into account the global features of their research topics and sites. One example of a new theme that emerged in the 1990s concerns trans-national forms of identification in the local-global interface. A very influential factor in this recent shift has been the introduction and fast acceptance of the Internet as a new means of communication, both among anthropologists and their informants (Lee 2003). Fieldwork is increasingly being complemented and even replaced by what may be called 'webwork', that is navigating the web in search of 'raw' ethnographic data in a hunter-and-gatherer way. The Internet has also facilitated the use of ethnography by informants and their former descendants, for instance in the Berber diaspora.

The Rifian Homeland

Immigrants from the Rif constitute approximately 80 percent of the total number of legal residents of Moroccan origin in the Netherlands. Most of them have both the Dutch and Moroccan nationality and many maintain ties with their region of origin.

The heart of northern Morocco consists of the Rif chain, until recently a typical frontier area with an erratic landscape, lack of roads, dispersed habitation, fragmented political structures and centuries of active resistance against outside interference. The mountain valleys and coastal zones are densely populated by sedentary Berbers who speak Tharafith. Agricultural yields are low (*Cannabis sativa* excepted) as a result of summer dryness, deforestation, erosion and poor soil. There are hardly alternative local means of subsistence apart from smuggling.

Until the establishment of the Spanish Protectorate over northern Morocco in 1912, the Rif area was a forgotten frontier, a 'land of dissidence' where piracy, banditry and tribal feuding were endemic. The Spanish who began to intrude the Rif during the last quarter of the nineteenth century were faced with fierce resistance by bands of tribal warriors. It took Protectorate Spain more than 15 years, heavy losses and French assistance to establish effective control over the central Rif area. As the Spanish withdrew in 1956, they left behind a deprived region with a deficient infrastructure and the highest population density of any mountainous area in the Mediterranean world.

Incorporated into the newly independent Moroccan kingdom, the administrative structure of the Rif was largely taken over by Arab civil servants from the cities of Atlantic Morocco. This, together with the closure of the Algerian border in 1956, triggered a Rifian revolt against the central government. For almost a century, border crossing with French Algeria had been of vital importance to the poor economy of the overpopulated Rif. Thousands of Rifi families were dependent on smuggling and seasonal labour migration to the large landed estates of western Algeria. The Moroccan army relentlessly crushed the hotbeds of the uprising. This defeat marked the beginning of mass labour migration of Rifians to Western Europe.

Rifian Ethnography

Apart from commercial and military penetration, Europeans also intruded on Rifian society by classifying and re-ordering it according to Western views. Elsewhere I have dealt with pre-colonial, colonial and post-colonial studies of the Rif (Driessen 1992: 55-78). The American anthropologist David M. Hart (1927-2001) stands out as the author of *The Aith Waryaghar of the Moroccan Rif* (1976), the most systematic, comprehensive and meticulous ethnographic study of a Rifian people. Hart did his main fieldwork during the last years of the Spanish Protectorate and the first of independent Morocco. His study is descriptive, holistic, with a strong focus on social structure and keen attention to ethnographic detail. The analytic emphasis is on pre-colonial blood-feuding and the Rifian model of segmentary descent and territoriality. The monograph bears a strong imprint of functionalism and a large part consists of historical reconstruction through interviews with old men. One drawback of this approach is the relegation of recent changes to a few final pages.

'The winds of change' have affected Rifian society in two fundamental respects. Firstly, there has been a rapid erosion of clan and tribe as basic forms of identification and organisation and an equally rapid rise of the individual and his or her nuclear family. This transformation is tied to the second major change, the progressive proletarianisation and labour nomadism of the former tribesmen. The impact of massive out-migration on the eastern Rif, is the topic of a more recent ethnography (McMurray 2001). Migration and smuggling have had the effect of devaluing all things local, including the obliteration of the collective memory and the loss of a heritage of resistance among the men who began to migrate to the Netherlands and Belgium in the early 1960s.

Ethnic Identification in Diaspora

The first generation of migrants from the Rif were known among Dutch employers as hard and obedient workers who rarely complained about working conditions, housing and pay. Until the late 1970s, there was a widespread believe among politicians and migrants themselves that the latter would return to their homelands. Quite on the contrary, the 1980s saw family reunion/formation and ethnicity building with a focus on Islam. State policy embraced multiculturalism. Together with the high concentration of Dutch Rifians in poor housing districts of large cities, this policy turned out to be an impediment to integration. Multiculturalism began to erode in the late 1990s when 'the problem of Moroccan adolescents' became manifest and leading political ideologists began to write about the 'multicultural drama' and Islam as a 'backward culture'.

It is against this background that 'Rifian culture' came to be blamed as a 'cause' of the assumed failure of integrating Moroccans into mainstream Dutch society and of the increase in violent and criminal behaviour among Moroccan adolescents. Anthropologist van Gemert (1998) pointed to a number of socio-economic factors and a key explanatory dimension defined as 'the reproduction of Rifian culture' which he derived from the historical ethnography on the Rif, in particular Hart's 1976 monograph.

Following the recent resurgence of radical Islam, the polarization of Muslims and non-Muslims after 9/11, and the murder of Theo van Gogh by a Muslim extremist of Rifian origin, the ethnic minority issue in the Netherlands became increasingly phrased in Islamic and anti-Islamic terms.

Redefining Berber Identity with *The Aith Waryaghar*

Hart's study was not only used by an anthropologist in the service of the government, but recently also by a new political movement aimed at young educated Moroccan Dutch largely living in The Hague and surrounding towns. The 'Voice of Moroccan Democrats in the Netherlands' ('Stem van Marokkaanse Democraten in Nederland', SMDN) points out that an increasing number of young Moroccans of the second and third generations are drawn to Islam as a major source of their identity. The vast majority of these new Dutch citizens hardly have any knowledge of their Rifian roots. In order to redress this ignorance, the SMDN sponsored the translation into Dutch of David Hart's *The Aith Waryaghar of the Moroccan Rif* with financial support of the municipality of The Hague.[8] The translation was prefaced by its mayor and is ambitiously claimed to be of general use in education, in particular in raising secular Berber consciousness among young people of Rifian origin. To stress this point, the first issue of the translation was offered to the Dutch Minister of Education.

One of the movement's spokespersons, Farid Aouled Lahcen, argued that a revival of Rifian culture among young men and women could serve as a counterpoise to Islamism and would undoubtedly strengthen the self-esteem of young Dutch Rifians, and consequently their integration into Dutch society. He claims a strong work ethic, self-discipline and perseverance as core Rifian values and rejects 'negative' customs such as giving daughters in marriage.[9] Does it come as a surprise that professional anthropologists are critical of such politically motivated selective readings of ethnography?

Conclusion

David Hart's ethnographic and historical knowledge is used by a small political movement as the ultimate source for Rifian values and the (re-)invention of a secular Rifian identity. I doubt whether Hart would have been pleased by this highly selective and opportunist way of celebrating frozen fragments of past Rifian culture and transporting them into a different time and space. He would certainly turn in his grave if he saw this Dutch edition with its misunderstandings of anthropological concepts, numerous mistakes and poor editing. His *Aith Waryaghar* would have deserved a more respectful and careful treatment as a source of knowledge and a posthumous reciprocal gift to the descendants of the original informants.

---

[8] D.M. Hart. 2007. *De Aïth Waryaghar van het Marokkaanse Rifgebied: Etnografie en geschiedenis* translated by C. Franken and S de Boer The Hague, Stem van de Marokkaanse Democraten in Nederland.

[9] Interview with F. A. Lahcen, *De Volkskrant* March 30, 2007. Also see http://www.tamazgha.nl.

References

Brettell, C.B. ed. 1993. *When They Read What We Write: The Politics of Ethnography* Westport, Bergin and Garvey.

Driessen, H. 1992. *On the Spanish-Moroccan Frontier: A Study in Ritual, Power and Ethnicity* Oxford, Berg.

Driessen, H. ed. 1993. *The Politics of Ethnographic Reading and Writing: Confrontations of Western and Indigenous Views* Saarbrücken, Breitenbach Publishers.

Gingrich, A. and R.G. Fox eds. 2002. *Anthropology, by Comparison* London, Routledge.

Hart, D.M. 1976. *The Aith Waryaghar of the Moroccan Rif: An Ethnography and History* New York and Tucson, Wenner Gren Foundation for Anthropological Research and University of Arizona Press.

Lee, H.M. 2003. *Tongans Overseas: Between Two Shores* Honolulu, University of Hawai'i Press.

McMurray, D.A. 2001. *In and Out of Morocco: Smuggling and Migration in a Frontier Boomtown* Minneapolis: University of Minnesota Press.

Van Gemert, F. 1998. *Ieder voor zich: Kansen, cultuur en criminaliteit van Marokkaanse jongens* Amsterdam, Het Spinhuis.

The Experience of the Elders: Learning Ethnographic Fieldwork in the Netherlands

Michael Fine

The scene is Riddershof[10] – a modern 140 bed nursing home in a large Dutch provincial city in the late 1970s. A young anthropologist from Australia is undertaking an ethnography of the nursing home and the Dutch welfare state. Using the methods of participant observation, and unable to be a resident he becomes a *leerling ziekeverzorgende* (trainee practical nurse) and commits to a two year vocational training program which involves a combination of supervised nursing care on the job supplemented by blocks of class room based education. In accordance with Dutch legislation, all those who work with the frail elderly and other vulnerable groups must be qualified or be in an educational training programme, their practice on the wards supervised by qualified staff.

Ethnographic research is essentially a process of learning social forms and cultural codes understood implicitly by insiders in an attempt to reveal them to other outsiders. It is an unspoken assumption of the participant observation methods employed that the most important information to be learned in the field can not be gleaned from books or other secondary sources but must be experienced first hand. The intangible, elusive and subjective component of personal experience is what distinguishes practical cultural competency from the awkward, bookish theoretical expertise that marks out the academic outsider from the adept insider. Learning some of the lessons of local history through experience shared with the elders, the supposed beneficiaries of the care provided in Riddershof, provided a powerful illustration of its importance.

---

[10] Riddershof is the pseudonym used for the nursing home to preserve the confidentiality of staff, residents and other participants in the study.

As part of the on-the-job apprenticeship involved in undertaking my first major field research project, I began to distinguish between three distinct but inter-related forms of learning. The first and perhaps most widely recognised technique of knowledge transmission concerned the processes of formal learning. Evidence of having followed such a process was necessary, for example, to demonstrate a level of professional competency amongst all nursing home staff as required under Dutch law. In this form, instruction took place according to an agreed curriculum which covered a range of generic educational competencies, which included basic mathematics, science and written Dutch, as well as the more specific clinical subjects required of practical nurses, such as anatomy, physiology and nursing practice. The results were confirmed through various forms of testing and exams, as well as through ongoing monitoring of daily practice on the wards. Clear criteria were established for demonstrating acceptable levels of competence. On the wards, for example, nursing tasks were graded from basic ones, such a bed making, for which mastery was required before work as a nurse could commence, through to more complex ones, such a giving intramuscular injections, that needed to be mastered in the second year of training so that the practitioner could work unsupervised. To ensure proficiency, *leerlingen* (student nurses) were required to carry a proficiency pass in which each of these tasks were listed. It was necessary for the student to undertake each of the tasks under supervision of a registered nurse and to receive a signature attesting to the attainment of professional competency on three occasions before she or he was permitted to undertake the task unsupervised. This practical monitoring of competencies on the ward was supplemented by a systematic and rigorous system of tests and annual exams administered as part of the block system of clinical education.

Formal education, in which learning was shaped by a curriculum imposed from above, was not confined to the teaching of students. Regular clinical updates for all professional staff were given on the wards covering a range of clinical topics, such as the dressing of wounds and advances in rehabilitation techniques. Unlike the educational component, however, there were no follow-up tests or exams for those attending these update sessions. Other forms of formal learning included the study of the Dutch language, which commenced at University in Australia where a reading course in Dutch was taught to students as part of the Indonesian Studies program and continued after arrival in the Netherlands through enrolment in a spoken Dutch language programme at the University of Nijmegen. But just as classroom learning on its own could not enable me to speak Dutch with any degree of proficiency, so too was formal learning insufficient to comprehend the complexity of the nursing home as a bureaucratically ordered residential setting for the frail aged.

Backing up, supporting and at the same time undermining the formal transfer of knowledge and behaviours, a second, informal and less tangible learning process operated. Informal learning took place in the process of interaction with others. Like formal learning it involved explicit instruction, but this was not constructed to follow a curriculum or approved programme of instruction. Although unplanned, its transmission was broader, taking place anywhere in the nursing home as well as beyond. Typically more important than the formal transmission of knowledge and competencies for the ethnographer, informal learning involved the communication of unwritten rules of conduct. Many of these were essential knowledge to enable staff to get the work finished in the time allotted. Informal instruction in these procedures generally took a particular form, where an older or more experience member of staff would simply say something like:

> Well, officially they teach you to do it this way, but here we have to be realistic. This is how it is really done, in practice. Everyone actually does it this way. Just don't ever tell anyone else.

Given their exclusion from the formal curriculum, residents, too, needed to resort to informal strategies of teaching and learning to train new staff members to their ways. As there was no history of intimate personal contact between individual staff members and the old aged residents of Riddershof, almost anything could become a matter of informal instruction. For example, how were the pillows to be propped up to ensure a comfortable night's rest? Where were the dentures to be placed so they could be fund the next morning in time for breakfast? There were also many other more profound lessons in life that residents sought to pass on. Some of these were social codes of conduct pertaining to expectations arising from Dutch culture. Others involved what might be termed 'local micro-knowledge' – peculiarities of the nursing home or ward such as the times of meals, the place that the blood pressure monitors are stored and the sitting places of each resident in the common lounge/dining room. Still others were more personal, pertaining for example to the habits, likes and dislikes of individual residents. Learning the unwritten rules of conduct by paying attention to the little details of life such as these was essential for the longer-term operation of the nursing home. It also had immediate importance for individuals concerned. Failure to recognise of the unique identity of each individual resident by ignoring their personal preferences, for example, could have considerable impact on their personal experience of receiving care with often quite profound and enduring effects.

A third, less immediately recognisable form of learning occurred through the accumulation of personal experience. This element of gaining knowledge is fundamental to the process of human learning, but is often overlooked by teachers and other pedagogical experts because the character of what is learned is so precarious and unpredictable. While I knew, in theory, that experience is central to the ethnographic method, its importance in the research process was driven home to me in a troubling incident that occurred one Sunday afternoon. It concerned an older resident who had seemed to be particularly isolated and who remarkably seemed to have little to do with most others in the nursing home, residents, staff and visitors alike.

I had been working on this ward for several weeks, gradually getting to know most of the residents and the peculiarities of their circumstances. One of the most senior men, De Heer L, allocated the privilege of a single room despite the absence of a medical condition that required his isolation, seemed particularly interesting. This was in no small part because he seemed to take such an active interest in Dutch and international politics. This afternoon he first asked, then demanded in an uncharacteristically aggressive tone, that I cease delivering afternoon tea to each of the residents and their visitors, my duties on the ward and give him my sole attention. I tried politely to decline, suggesting that I would be back with him as soon as I had finished helping the few remaining residents, when he turned on me and began shouting, holding his fist high in what was unmistakably a physical threat.

'Get back to your own country, jew boy, you useless, disgusting little foreigner' he screamed.

His words could be heard throughout the ward, as he continued to denounce me. I sought to reason, but he continued, so I withdrew, humiliated, shutting the door behind me. On this occasion, my attempt to observe while passing as one of the participants, had obviously failed.

On the ward other residents who had heard the incident turned to me, offering their apologies and consolation and reluctantly filling me in on the unspoken history they each knew about but had been too polite to pass on. Meneer L was known by the older people throughout the city as a Nazi sympathiser and collaborator during the second world war. Until that moment, their experience was something they had not needed to share. Now, I too knew what they knew and could deport myself accordingly.

On Hermeneutics,
Ad's Antennas
and the Wholly Other

René van der Haar

Ad Borsboom's *De clan van de Wilde Honing*, i.e. *'The Sugarbag Clan'* has as its subtitle *Spiritual Wealth of the Aborigines*. In the context of an orientalist world-view, this title would certainly appeal to the imagination while positioning the Western subject and the Aboriginal object in two distinct worlds. The cover layout with its illustration of barefoot prints underneath the subtitle, and a picture of a blue sky with dark-skinned children looking into the bright light of the sun, seems only to underscore this interpretation. We, the post-industrial Western readers, are pursuing our ever-increasing material needs in our murky wasteland. They, the ones under scrutiny, are following the path charted by their spiritual ancestors in their bright and unblemished southland. The actual text of the book confirms the dichotomy already expected:

> As an outsider, you do not really notice it at first, but slowly it starts to dawn on you: you can no longer escape. Everything around you is alive: the ground you sleep on, the grass you walk on, the woods and the water where you search for food. There is movement everywhere; there are sounds everywhere. The nights are quieter, but that tranquillity is no less penetrating. Very soon you are no longer aware of the countless mosquitoes that become active after sunset. But, unnoticed, their buzzing sounds are always there in the background; it even makes the tranquillity vibrate with life. [...] Is it surprising that people who have lived for centuries in such an environment experience the world around them as a spirited one (117)?

My own world is so different. Ninety percent of our environment consists of lifeless matter and implements that we have made ourselves. Apart from a drooping plant, the room in which I am putting my experiences in writing consists of lifeless matter: a computer, furniture, stone walls, and books. To a large extent, our daily environment has been created by ourselves. There is no mystery, no higher power. The lifeless matter does not invoke any feelings of spiritual connectedness and dependence at all (119-20).

The culture, which Ad Borsboom describes, that of the Djinang people, is of the type that was particularly popular subject matter in the heyday of ethnography. The linguist and anthropologist Edward Sapir identifies this type of culture thus:

The genuine culture is not necessary either high or low; it is merely inherently harmonious, balanced and self-satisfactory. It is the expression of a richly varied and yet somehow unified and consistent attitude toward life, an attitude, which sees the significance of any one element of civilization in its relation to all others. It is, ideally speaking, a culture in which nothing is spiritually meaningless, in which no important part of the general functioning brings with it a sense of frustration, or misdirected or unsympathetic effort (Sapir 1924: 410, cited in Levy 2005: 438).

I would argue that Sapir's description does not cover an entire culture. His words apply only to the cultural part of a culture, the order of accomplishments; not the natural part of a culture, the order of passions. Ad Borsboom defines the cultural part of the culture of the Djinang people as follows:

The life cycle of every person born in the Sugarbag clan is inextricably bound to the cycle of Djaware. This creature is every member's origin and ultimate destination. To everyone who has originated from it, it provides the orientation and identity during his/her lifetime (105).

Its footprints can be read in the soil; they can also be retraced in the stories and songs that it has left behind. They provide every generation with a blueprint for life, and see to it that people do not get lost, neither literally, in the country, nor figurative, on the sometimes confusing path through life (120).

In an earlier passage he briefly mentions the natural part of the culture of the people described, although it is not very clear in what period of time the things he describes occured:

> Aboriginal communities and the people that form them need not be idealized; they were and are only human. The distrust of strangers, the belief in black magic, deadly acts of vengeance when others were suspected of magic, severe physical punishment for the violation of certain taboos, mutual abduction of potential wedding partners and the subsequent blood feuds – they were all part of everyday human behaviour (35).

What is this 'richly varied and yet somehow unified and consistent attitude towards life' in the case of the Sugarbag clan? What attitude to life causes the Djinang culture to be not an arbitrary bundle of survival strategies or a mindless machine, but a spiritually consistent way of life? To my mind, this attitude can be found both hermeneutically and empathically.

Apart from being an expert methodology, hermeneutics are part of our every-day routines. At any moment of the day, we have to determine – aided by indications from our environment and from ourselves – what our present situation is, what rules apply to that particular situation, what our intentions are, what strategies can be followed to comply with these rules and intentions, and what actions we are actually going to take. When we apply this framework to our bond with another person, not by circling between the pieces of the jigsaw and the picture as a whole, which is what happens in the hermeneutic process, but all at once, in one go, this is called empathy. The foundation for successfully empathizing with other people is said to be the 'seelische Lebendigkeit' that everyone shares (Dilthey 1924 [1900]: 334, cited in Van der Harst 1989: 100).

Although I know Ad Borsboom to be a man of great empathic powers, a man equipped with a great many social antennae, he complains in his book about the thick crust of western rationality that for a long time prevented him from understanding the members of the clan (115). I would rather propose that these two, rationality and empathy, are not opposing forces. One sets out to meet the other rationally, plodding away hermeneutically, learning the hard way, as described above, as long as one's level of knowledge does not allow for an empathic (unconsciously informed) jump.

On the basis of Ad Borsboom's information in *The Sugarbag Clan* I think that the 'richly varied and yet somehow consistent attitude toward life', which makes the Djinang culture a spiritually consistent way of life, is made up of 'the spiritual connection and dependence' that these people feel for their environment, which to them is life itself. For this formulation, I refer to the second of the aforementioned citations from Ad Borsboom's book.

In the first quotation, Ad Borsboom asks us to empathize in two steps with someone in a situation of complete immersion in the natural world of Australia. First he asks us to empathize with him, living in the Australian bush, and then, through him, to empathize with the Aborigines for whom this way of life in the not-too-distant past was all they knew. I think that we can attain this, not only because of the fact that we probably are kindred spirits, but also, in connection with and as a continuation of this, because in our past lifetime, in moments of intense susceptibility, we were able to experience a qualitatively adequate perception of nature. There was a time when we did not look miserably at a pathetic little plant next to a computer. There was a time when a simple flower could be the whole world, and more, by which I mean the wholly other. The priest and poet Gerard Manley Hopkins phrases such a moment as follows:

> I do not think I have ever seen anything more beautiful than the bluebell I have been looking at. I know the beauty of our Lord by it. Its inscape is mixed of strength and grace like an ash tree. The head is strongly drawn over backwards and arched down like a cutwater drawing itself back from the line of the keel. The lines of the bell strike and overlie this, rayed but not symmetrically, some lie parallel (Hopkins 1959 [1870]: 199, cited in Knight and Mason 2006: 109-10).

In accordance with this quotation, I think the key to the spiritual, the wholly other, is the ability to pay complete attention to the non-human other, which is nature. And the memory of such a moment of transition will probably contribute, in my opinion, to the understanding of the non-familiar human other, which is the other person who not only focuses on, but is also guided by the spiritual. So to learn and to understand is partly to remember and to realise what we already knew.

References

Borsboom, A. 1996. *De clan van de Wilde Honing: Spirituele rijkdom van de Aborigines [The Sugarbag Clan: Spiritual Wealth of the Aborigines]* Haarlem, Becht.

Knight, M. and E. Mason. 2006. *Nineteenth-Century Religion and Literature: An Introduction* Oxford, Oxford University Press.

Levy, R.I. 2005. 'Ethnography, Comparison, and Changing Times' *Ethos* 33, 4: 435-458.

Van der Harst, J. 1989. *Verklaring en interpretatie in de literatuurwetenschap* Amsterdam, University of Amsterdam, PhD thesis.

Bontius in Batavia: Early Steps in Intercultural Communication

Frans Hüsken

After having been dependent upon the Sultan of Banten for more than a decade, the Dutch East India Company (VOC), or rather its governor general Jan Pieterszoon Coen, decided in 1617 to build their own premises at the place where present-day North Jakarta is located. A map of 1627 shows that Batavia, as the new town was called, was basically a fortress and a walled area with warehouses and residences. It had no more than five to six thousands inhabitants, including some 700 Dutchmen, a multi-ethnic garrison, many Chinese and slaves from all over Asia. They lived in a town that was built in Dutch fashion. That meant canals for the transportation of merchandise, compact buildings for offices and living quarters, and inevitably, windmills and draw bridges. As the settlers were soon to find out, under tropical conditions the houses proved to be suffocating and the canals pestilentious as well as an agreeable home to local crocodiles.

The new town faced a series of major challenges. First of all, attacks from Javanese princes, in particular Sultan Agung of the mighty Central Javanese principality of Mataram, who wanted the Dutch out of their way. The settlers could handle that, be it with great pains. But there were other threats. The major one was the high mortality among them caused by little-known or unknown tropical diseases. Figures for those years vary between sources but 10-20 per cent of the European population died within a couple of years, often months, after arrival.[11] Most of the survivors suffered more or less chronically from malaria, cholera, *beriberi*, rash and skin infections and many other diseases. Contemporary European medicine was ineffective as it did know nothing about possible causes, and thus

---

[11] A century later, the situation would be even worse with about half of the VOC military dying within six months after their arrival in Batavia. Cf. P.H. van der Brug. 1997. 'Malaria in Batavia in 18th Century' *Tropical Medicine and International Health* 2, 9: 892-902

prevention, and next to nothing about their treatment. Better ways of coping with these tropical plagues were urgently needed.

Batavia's founder and VOC governor-general Coen asked the Amsterdam office for assistance and the urgent arrival of competent medical doctors. One of them was Jacob Bontius (1592-1631), a young man who had recently graduated from the equally young University of Leiden. With not much more than fundamental knowledge of European medicine, and a book by the Portuguese physician Garcia de Orta, he arrived in 1627 in Batavia. All in all, he lived there for not more than four years. From the start he himself suffered from malaria, dysentery, and *beriberi*. If that in itself is a indication of the unhealthy Batavian environment of the 1620s, the more so the fact that his second wife died (he had lost his first wife already on their way to the Indies) as well as two of his children, and that he saw some good friends, including the Governor General pass away in those four years. Eventually, in 1631 Bontius himself fell victim to the 'killer germs of the tropics'.

Bontius was not primarily employed as a physician. His official position was that of *advocaat-generaal* (attorney general) and bailiff of Batavia; and he was the *archiater* (chief physician, apothecary and surgical inspector) of the town. Those positions apparently left him with enough time to collect botanical data – tropical plants being very much in fashion in Europe – and to note down the ways these were used in indigenous therapies. He wrote four, often extensive, treatises that were all published after his death. His main work *De Medicina Indorum* (On the Medicine of the Indies) came out in Leiden in 1642, and has been reprinted and translated many times since.[12]

Bontius did not start from scratch but could rely on the book of Garcia da Orta that he brought along on his trip. Orta had lived in Goa (India) and his *Coloquios dos simples e drogas he Cousas medicinais da India* came out in 1563. This work was based upon his longstanding contacts with Ayurvedic and Ezhava specialists who were his main informants on botanical and pharmacological matters. He acknowledged their views as representing equivalent medical epistemologies,

---

[12] This section relies heavily on the work by R. Grove 1996. 'Indigenous Knowledge and the Significance of South-West India for the Portuguese and Dutch Construction of Tropical Nature' *Modern Asian Studies* 30, 1: 121-143.

next to the much better-known European and Arabic traditions. In fact, as Grove put it, the *Coloquios* was profoundly 'an early exercise in ethnobotany'.

Like Orta, Bontius stressed that traditional European scholastic medicine was of little use in the tropics, and like Orta, he started to look for indigenous sources of botanical and medical knowledge in Batavia. He contacted a number of indigenous men and women who were said to know about illness and healing and about the plants that could be used to cure the rampant diseases of the East like malaria, dysentery, jaundice, cholera and *beriberi*. In his *De Medicina Indorum* he presented the profiles of these diseases, giving their local names, symptoms, possible causes and treatments. As the areas outside Batavia were still considered to be unsafe territory for Europeans where they could be attacked by hostile Javanese or by wild animals, Bontius could not collect plants himself, but 'friendly natives' brought him material from even the remote parts of the island.

To the modern reader, who is used to colonial racism and its contempt of the superstition and stupidity of 'natives', Bontius views may come as a surprise. He generously acknowledged his debt to these medical practitioners to whom he turned for advice as their methods and medicines proved to be far more effective in treating the diseases than any method known in Western medicine.

Just a few quotations from Bontius' work prove not only his respect for his teachers, but also his disdain of the Dutch VOC staff that just saw Asians as uncivilised and barbarous:

> I often marvel at the carelessness of our people, who without respect call these people barbarians, although not only in their knowledge of herbs but in all aspects if their economic system leave our own far behind.

And further on:

> Every Malay woman practices medicine and midwifery so well that – I confess that it is the case – I would prefer to submit myself to such hands than to a half-taught doctor or arrogant surgeon,

whose shadow of an education was acquired in schools, being inflated with presumption while having no real experience.[13]

After his death, Bontius became well known through his description of the clinical pictures of some nineteen main tropical diseases, particularly that of *beriberi* (from which he suffered himself), a paralytic form of polyneuropathy:

> A certain very troublesome affliction, which attacks men, is called by the inhabitants *Beriberi* (which means sheep). I believe those, whom this same disease attacks, with their knees shaking and legs raised up, walk like sheep. It is a kind of paralysis, or rather Tremor: for it penetrates the motion and sensation of the hands and feet indeed sometimes the whole body...

The patient loses weight, is emotionally disturbed, his sensory perceptions are impaired; a general weakness of the body and pain in the limbs; irregular heart beat and oedema; in severe cases the disease may lead to heart failure and death.

Bontius' interest in and description of *beriberi* has earned him the epitheton of being 'the founder of tropical medicine'. This may be a bit over the top as with equal merits the title might have gone to Orta, working in Goa, and Van Reede tot Drakenstein who was active as a botanist in the VOC *factory* in Malabar (South India).[14] But for the Dutch tradition of tropical medical research Bontius has been of special importance as his early description of *beriberi* had successful follow-ups. Shortly after Bontius's death, the then famous Dr Nicolaes Tulp (who became even more famous after Rembrandt painted him at the centre of his 'Anatomy Lesson') continued upon the aetiology of *beriberi*. But it was several centuries later that *beriberi* research led to the discovery of the role of vitamins through the work of a number

---

[13] Translated quotations are taken from the inaugural address of H. Cook. 2003 (27 February). *Medicine, Materialism, Globalism: The Example of the Dutch Golden Age* London, University College London.

[14] On Van Reede see: J. Heniger. 1986. *Hendrik Adriaan van Reede tot Drakenstein (1636-1691) and Hortus Malabaricus: A Contribution to the History of Dutch Colonial Botany* Rotterdam, Balkema.

of Dutch researchers, one of whom was awarded the Nobel Prize in 1929. And again in that case it was an unknown Indonesian who, unwittingly, made a decisive contribution.

In the 19th century, *beriberi* continued to have a high incidence in the Netherlands Indies, and in particular among soldiers of the colonial army and prison inmates. The Dutch government therefore stimulated research into its causes. Christiaan Eijkman (1858-1930) was one in a line of researchers trying to tackle the disease. His case is a classic example of the role of a lucky accident in scientific research. In his experiments he injected chickens with blood and urine of *beriberi* patients; after a while, they developed the same symptoms that the patients had. But unexpectedly, also the chickens that had not been treated, contracted the disease. 'Eijkman's attention was serendipitously drawn to the coincidence that the chickens no longer developed *polyneuritis gallinarum*[15] after being fed crude uncooked rice instead of the polished rice from the Military Hospital's kitchen. The new cook, a stickler for Army regulations, refused to give "military rice to civilian hens".[16] All sick chickens recovered when they were fed unhusked rice. So it transpired to him that it was the polished white rice that was responsible for *polyneuritis*, and that something in the bran and germ of the unhusked rice protected them from and cured the disease.

That observation led to further research and experiments with dietary changes in which human patients were given meat and vegetables instead of cooked white rice. It turned out to be a major breakthrough in *beriberi* research that finally led to the discovery of vital amino acids, or vitamins, in the rice husks. It was ironic that without the knowledge of the role of vitamins but based upon the practical experience of his Indonesian teachers, Bontius had given a similar

---

[15] In order to study *beriberi* Eijkman concentrated upon degeneration of the peripheral nerves (*polyneuritis*) which is a prominent and painful symptom of human *beriberi*.

[16] G.W. Bruyn and C.M. Poser. 2003. *The History of Tropical Neurology: Nutritional Disorders* Nantucket, Science History Publications: 9.

advice on the diet of *beriberi* patients but that his remarks had been forgotten.[17]

But can Bontius be called 'a major founder of tropical medicine'? One could deny that as all his knowledge came from the anonymous Javanese, Sundanese and/or Chinese teachers and practitioners who initiated him in their tradition of knowledge. On the other hand, it was Bontius who wrote and commented upon their knowledge and who started to accumulate, systematize and synthesize their information in his *De Medicina Indorum*, thereby turning the Asian pharmacopoeia into a powerful tool to cope with a whole range of debilitating or fatal diseases. From that, and from the other manuscripts that were published after his death, others could build and start experimenting, even if the development of tropical medicine does not follow a unilinear evolutionary path and often older knowledge was forgotten. Bontius' informants could not have done this alone. But rather than being a victory of Western science, the tropical medicine that we have today is the outcome of a synergy and blending of two medical traditions. However, what strikes the eye is that in the historiography Western researchers receive all the credits while the contributions of Asian medical specialists are not acknowledged. In those rare cases that they are, those who brought their views forward enter history as 'friendly natives' but have no names – like, in the lines of Bertold Brecht's Mack-the-Knife song:

Und die einen sind im Dunkeln
Und die anderen sind im Licht
Doch man sieht nur die im Lichte
Die im Dunkeln sieht man nich

---

[17] Rumphius (1627-1702), a merchant living in the Moluccas and highly interested in botany, had given an even better dietary advice to cure beriberi by feeding the patients with mungo beans (*Kacang ijo*). But also his comments had been forgotten two centuries later. See I. Snapper. 1945. 'Medical Contributions from the Netherlands Indies' eds. P. Honig and F. Verdoorn *Science and Scientists in the Netherlands Indies* New York, Board of the Netherlands Indies, Surinam and Curaçao: 312-313. It might well have been the excessive self-confidence of modern medicine in the 19th century that made it forget or discard their 17th century predecessors as they relied too much on 'unscientific' native sources.

Ceremonies of Learning and Status in Jordan

Willy Jansen

Graduation Rituals in Jordan

The class of 2006 was nervously waiting in the foyer, while their family and friends passed the security check and found a place in Amman's Cultural Palace. The 76 female graduates had undergone a complete make-over. Their brown, baggy school uniform had been replaced by a black and red gown and cap; all had visited a beautician and hair stylist and bought new high-heeled black pumps. The girls far outshone and outnumbered the 42 boys. The elite of Jordan's capital had gathered here for the graduation ceremony of two of the oldest and best private secondary schools, the Ahliyya School for Girls and the Bishop School for Boys. Like Jordan's other private schools founded by Christians in the 20th century, they serve not only the very small Christian minority (approx. 5%), but also the Muslim elite. Soon after the graduates had proudly walked onto the stage under loud cheering of family and friends, Her Royal Highness Princess Basma Bint Talal entered under loud applause.

Graduation rituals are important markers of the educational career of Jordanians. Secondary schools and universities, in particular the private ones, stage elaborate rituals to mark the stages of knowledge gathering of their students. I participated in a number of them in 1989 and 2006, and collected information on several more. The data revealed three characteristics: the presence of royalty, the high expenditure on such rituals, and the publicity around them. I will describe and analyze these characteristics to gain insight in what is actually being transmitted during these rituals. I will argue that it is not only knowledge that is celebrated, but just as much social status. This is most clearly shown in the education of girls, who are not educated for the labour market but for the status of their family.

Royal patronage was very noticeable in this graduation ceremony. On my formal invitation card the name of the patron Princess Basma

Bint Talal was printed in the largest letter type. In the school's year book a picture of King Abdullah adorned the first page, followed by one of Princess Basma on the second. In the speeches held by the directors of the two schools the names of Princess Basma and her brother the late King Hussein were frequently mentioned, each time leading to clapping and cheers by the public. The Princess took the honorable role of handing the diploma to each student. Also other schools and universities have close ties with specific members of the royal family and use royal symbols in their self-representations. Especially Prince Hassan Bin Talal is frequently referred to as he has done much for the elevation of Jordanian education, in particular at secondary and university level, and for promoting academic excellence. Prince Hassan is the brother of late king Hussein. He chairs the Higher Council for Science and Technology as well as the Board of Trustees for the Royal Scientific Society. He instituted the El-Hassan Bin Talal Award for Academic Excellence and his wife Sarvath Al-Hassan chairs the Award Committee. The couple is also involved in the Amman Baccalaureate School, previously called the Prince Hassan School. The Jordanian newspaper *The Star* of June 8, 2006 showed that the Prince patronized the school's graduation ceremony. One university, the Princess Sumaya University for Technology, is named after Hassan's daughter. The Princess is deputy chair of its Board of Trustees.

At every major graduation ceremony in Jordan a member of the royal family is present, and schools pride themselves in having good connections with at least one family member who is preferably as close to the throne as possible. The Rosary College usually welcomes Princess Alia. In 2006 she addressed its 132 graduates. She went to the Rosary school herself, just like Princess Aisha and Princess Zayna (two other daughters of King Hussein) and Princess Taghrid (wife of Hussein's brother). The Jubilee School in Amman, specialized in education for gifted children, was called after the Silver Jubilee of King Hussein's accession to the throne. It was one of the undertakings of the Queen Noor Al-Hussein Foundation. In 2005, its diplomas were handed out by Prince Hamza Bin al-Hussein, eldest son of King Hussein and Queen Noor. *The Star* (June 8, 2006) also reported that the graduation ceremony at the Montessori school was presided over by Prince Faysal Bin al-Hussain (brother of the present king), that of the Al-Quds College by Princess Basma Bint Talal (aunt of the king) and that of the Sa'adah School by Princess Alia Al-Faysal (half sister of the king). Royal patronage of education is clearly present in Jordanian society. In the graduation ritual, royal charisma is disseminated by proximity and touching.

The expenditure lavished on the graduation ceremony, in dressing the graduate, paying for the pictures, the year book, and the parties leading after the ceremony, is high. It comes on top of the already high costs of private education and of the sports activities, holiday outings, cultural meetings and trips private schools organize as extra attraction of their education. Parents pride themselves on not complaining of the costs. One mother said: 'There are families who eat nothing in order to let their children go to school.' In the graduation rituals and the other public events of the schools it is publicly shown that these parents are willing to make these sacrifices.

Not only royalty and expenditure, but also publicity characterizes graduations. My invitation card stated that 'Cameras are not allowed', but many parents and friends disregarded this. Several professional photographers and film makers produced visual memories of the ceremony. Following the American example, also official graduation pictures are taken of each candidate in cap and gown. Royalty, public celebrations and publicity are closely connected. When the member of the royal family hands over the diplomas an official picture is taken. The graduate will cherish and frame in particular this photograph that proves his or her proximity to royalty. Many treat it with more respect than the graduation portrait. For years to come it will decorate the living room, and parents and grandparents will retain another copy in their house to show to family and friends. The presence of royalty guarantees that newspapers will pay attention to graduation ceremonies.

Celebrating Knowledge or Celebrating Status?

Why do royalty, lavish expenditure and ostentatious presentation take such a prominent place in graduation ceremonies? First it indicates a pervasive respect for education in Jordanian culture. This is not recent, but based on a long tradition of respect for literacy, learning and intellectual authority (Shryock 1997: 245). These rituals celebrate knowledge and learning. Yet, they seem to celebrate also something else. Authors like Bourdieu, have noted before how higher education distinguishes different categories of people, and how social status is being reproduced by the school system (Bourdieu 1989). The school system, and in particular a private school system, not only transmits knowledge and creates opportunities for social ascension, but it may also reproduce existing inequalities. It transmits a form a cultural capital that encompasses more than just school knowledge. That also Jordanian parents realise this can be seen from the fact that more groups than expected send their children to private schools, although private schools are not necessarily better than state schools.

They justify this expenditure by saying that they want to prepare their children for a good job, but this argument only holds for boys. Contrary to Western expectations, Jordanian parents positively encourage schooling of daughters and show a remarkable willingness to pay for an expensive higher education for them (Jansen 2006). Yet, many forbid their daughters to use this education in a paid job, leading to much frustration among the highly educated young women who resent the gossip and harassment and the concern with their reputation that hinders them in taking a public role (Droeber 2005: 70-71). Highly educated women do work somewhat more often than uneducated women, but are also more often unemployed (Hanssen-Bauer 1998). The unproductive expenditure on female education serves the same function as royal patronage, lavish celebrations and public visibility: it enhances the respect for and status of the family as it shows that the family is able to function economically and socially well in this higher stratum of society, and it increases the chances of a good marriage for the girl. Veblen (1899) already showed that conspicuous consumption by dressing up women and servants reflected and fortified the position of the husband or father. Dressing the daughter in a graduation gown sends out messages about the wealth and status of the family.

Moreover, receiving one's diploma out of the hands of royalty, and being able to prove royal patronage in the graduation picture, reflects and reinforces one's social status. It expresses the new social capital obtained with the degree as one now is seen to figure in the highest circles of society. The visual proofs of this status, the pictures, news-paper announcements, year book and DVD, form a permanent cultural capital to draw upon in the future. But not only the graduates and their families gain status. Through the graduation ceremonies, royalty and the cultural capital of diplomas mutually constitute each other. Each profit from the status obtained.

REFERENCES

Bourdieu, P. 1989. *La noblesse d'état: Grandes écoles et esprit de corps* Paris, Éditions de Minuit.

Droeber, J. 2005. *Dreaming of Change: Young Middle-Class Women and Social Transformation in Jordan* Leiden, Brill.

Hanssen-Bauer, J., J. Pedersen and A.A. Tiltnes eds. 1998. *Jordanian Society: Living Conditions in the Hashemite Kingdom of Jordan* Toyen, Fafo Institute for Applied Social Science.

Jansen, W. 2006. 'Gender and the Expansion of University Education in Jordan' *Gender and Education* 18, 5: 473-489.

Shryock, A. 1997. *Nationalism and the Genealogical Imagination: Oral History and Textual Authority in Tribal Jordan* Berkeley, University of California Press.

Veblen, T.B. 1994 [1899]. *Theory of the Leisure Class* Mineola, Dover Publications.

Al Amien: A Modern Variant of an Age-Old Educational Institution

Huub de Jonge

The *pesantren* or Islamic boarding school is thought to be the oldest Islamic educational institution in Indonesia. Most of them are situated in the countryside and in particular attract students, *santris*, from peasant, fishermen and traders circles. In principle, these schools constitute a kind of religious community in which children and youngsters immerse themselves deeply in the study of Islam and learn to live as good Muslims. Outsiders often see the pesantren as an anachronism. The writer Naipaul (1981: 317), for example, describes it as a type of schooling appropriate to a time in which villagers seldom crossed local boundaries and the 'pesantren preserved the harmony between community and school, village life and education.' However, as an institution 'to duplicate the village atmosphere, to teach villagers to be villagers' (ibid.: 341), he considers these schools out of place in a modernizing world. Some Indonesians I met, both Muslims and non-Muslims, would agree with Naipaul, sometimes calling the pesantrens hotbeds of Islamic fanaticism. In saying this they often referred to those that spurred up violence in the country, protesting against processes of westernisation, or to those that sided with the Taliban in Afghanistan. These comments, however, give a distorted and a less than subtle picture of the Islamic boarding schools that ignores the fact that most pesantrens are peaceful places of study that try to adapt to the demands of the time. They also ignore the reality that the pesantren has become a competitor to be reckoned with to formal, mostly government run schools. I shall illustrate this on the basis of the history of the pesantren Al Amien, located in the village of Prenduan on the island of Madura, where I did fieldwork in the second half of the 1970s and to which I have returned several times.

The pesantren Al Amien (The Trustworthy) was officially founded in 1972, though it had long existed under a different name before then. Its predecessor dated from the end of the 19th century and was led by a *kyai* or Islamic teacher called Chotib. This man was the grandfather of the three kyais who made Al Amien a renowned centre of learning in East Java and beyond at the end of the 20th century. As elsewhere in Indonesia, kyai Chotib's pesantren consisted of a small prayer house, supplemented with the dwelling of the kyai and bamboo huts for a small number of male students. Seated in front of a half circle of santris on the floor of the prayer house, the kyai gave daily lectures on various religious subjects. In form, the pesantren's style of teaching closely resembled the way knowledge was transferred between teachers and students in the preceding Hindu-Buddhist period. Besides receiving a religious education, the students learned to be self-reliant and persistent. Just as they do today, the santris kept their own living quarter in order, cooked their own food, and cared for their own possessions. In the past they also cultivated their own food crops though nowadays their daily necessities are bought with money donated by parents or sponsors. Just as places of education in pre-Islamic times, the pesantrens were built amid fields given by worldly benefactors. Most santris did not spend more than a few years studying with an Islamic teacher, as they were badly needed at home to help to make a living.

After Chotib died in 1939, his position in the pesantren was taken over by his son Jauhari, who was educated at several pesantrens in Java and had even studied in Mecca for a few years. Inspired by the education policy of nationalist oriented Islamic organisations like Muhammadiyah and Nahdlatul Ulama, Jauhari decided to drastically reorganize the method of instruction by introducing classroom teaching. However, these plans were delayed by the Japanese occupation and the struggle for independence. It was only in 1952 that he was able to start two *madrasah*, Islamic primary schools, one for boys and one for girls, where besides Islamic topics a small number of secular subjects was taught. The madrasah's, which were attended by both resident and non-resident pupils, were such a success that within a few years two more schools were opened.

Kyai Jauhari was a progressive person and one of the few religious leaders in Madura to send his three sons to the pesantren Darrussa-laam (Place of Peace) in Gontor, East Java. This latter boarding school is still one of the most important Islamic centres of learning in Indo-nesia. The curriculum of this so-called *pesantren moderen* differs significantly from that of more conservative boarding schools. School life is more disciplined, teaching more systematized, and much atten-tion is paid to worldly subjects. Besides Indonesian, lessons are given in Arabic and English. The school has a strong international orienta-tion and every year a number of students have the opportunity to continue their studies at foreign universities.

In 1972, a year after kyai Jauhari died, his brother and sisters and their descendants took over the running of his madrasahs. Jauhari's eldest son, Tijani, opened the pesantren Al Amien, which was fully based on the Gontor-model and which at first concentrated on the education of religious teachers for primary and secondary schools. Kyai Tijani, who had married a daughter of the leader of pesantren Darrussalaam, knew how to set about his work. Within a year he built a completely new pesantren amidst the rice fields outside the village, consisting of a mosque, a school, a dormitory, and houses for himself and his brothers, who had also started to function as kyais. The purchase of six hectares of land and the construction of the buildings was financed through donations from former santris and local philanthropists. Local tobacco traders, who were making fortunes in the 1970s, were extremely generous and did not want to be outdone by each other.

In the following years Al Amien was expanded with junior and senior secondary schools and an institute for higher Islamic studies that later gained the status of a theological college. The number of students increased yearly and later also included girls who, at the secondary levels, where educated separately. The first year the pesantren had 46 santris from the village of whom eleven finished school. In 1977, when I resided in Prenduan, Al Amien had 125 students, among whom several from Java. In 2000 the number of santris, who now came from all over Indonesia, had increased to more than 5000 and the number of alumni had risen to about 2000.

It would be too easy to ascribe the success of the three kyais, the triumvirate that leads the pesantren, to the revival of Islam that Indonesia has experienced since the 1990s. However, I think it more significant that, in contrast to its predecessors, Al Amien gives its students increased opportunities for upward social mobility. The schooling gives the santris a chance to escape the meagre living they might make on the infertile island of Madura. During Soeharto's New Order, the kyais complied with the directives of both the Department of Religious Affairs and the Department of Education, despite all kinds of objections against the nature of the regime. This gave the students the opportunity to continue their studies at higher levels of Islamic and secular education. Without neglecting typical Islamic subjects like Islamic history and culture, Islamic law, Islamic ethics, and the Arabic language, they extended the curriculum with prescribed secular subjects, appointed qualified teachers in those fields, and agreed to deliver development-minded persons who would be as employable as students with a purely secular education.

Since Soeharto's resignation and the start of the era of reformation (*reformasi*), the pesantren has profited from all kinds of national and regional measures that slightly (or greatly, as some would have it) favour Islamic education. For the first time in Indonesian history, the pesantren, a non-formal educational institution, is now legally recognized. Within the framework of the decentralization policy it is stipulated that: 'society has the right to organise society-based education for formal and non-formal purposes in accordance with religious, socio-environmental and cultural characteristics for the sake of the interests of society' (Ichwan 2006: 293). This allows greater leeway for the preservation and accentuation of local characteristics that the previous regime did.

The open-minded and practical attitude of the kyais has done Al Amien no harm. It now occupies an area of 20 ha and has the most modern facilities at its disposal, including a language laboratory and an excellent library, which were partly paid for by Saudi-Arabian sources. A growing, largely self-trained staff does the teaching. An increase in Islamic colleges and universities has allowed more and more alumni to move to advanced levels of education and obtain higher positions in society. Several former students have continued their studies in the Middle East or in the United States. The kyais, who now have the status of *ulama*, Muslim scholars, are much sought-after guests at conferences and forums on radio and television. Every now and then they are consulted on social affairs by worldly authorities.

One of the striking characteristics of the old type of pesantren was the close personal relationship between kyai and santri. Due to the tremendous increase in the number of students this has become almost impossible. Most santris, however, still consider the kyai to be an important guide in their lives. They draw upon the kyai's knowledge and carry what they learned from him with them for the rest of their careers. Other centuries-old features, however, have hardly changed. As in the past, the boarding school still functions as a relatively autonomous religious community in which Islamic norms and values are cherished, and harmony and solidarity dominate.

REFERENCES

Ichwan, M.N. 2006. *Official Reform of Islam: State Islam and the Ministry of Religious Affairs in Contemporary Indonesia, 1966-2004* Tilburg, Universiteit van Tilburg, PhD thesis.

Naipaul, V.S. 1981. *Among the Believers: An Islamic Journey* New York, Alfred A. Knopf.

Yolngu and Anthropological Learning Styles in Ritual Contexts

Ian Keen

Early researchers on Yolngu learning styles pointed out that the pervasive Yolngu approach to learning is by means of observation and participation rather than through formal instruction (e.g. Harris 1984). A girl (or woman visitor from another culture) learning to twine baskets, for example, will sit with knowledgeable women, observing and trying to copy their technique. From time to time a woman will take the novice's work, continue it, and then hand it back (e.g. Hamby 2001); there is little instruction as such. The clash between Yolngu learning styles and schooling is evident – Yolngu children treat school rather as a kind of ritual, such that mere participation was thought sufficient to be schooled (Christie 1984).

This style of learning is evident in *garma* ('public') ceremonies, which incorporate *bunggul* (dance) and *manikay* (songs using clapsticks and didgeridoo) genres. Male singers sit in a group, each equipped with a pair of ironwood clapsticks, and normally accompanied by a single didgeridoo player. The Marradjirri ceremony of Djinang people, described by Borsboom in his PhD thesis (1978), is of this kind. The songs consist of a sequence of topics, each realised by a number of song items each a few minutes in length. The singers perform the melody more or less in unison, but extemporise the text, drawing on a stock of words and phrases appropriate to the topic and the occasion, rather as a jazz player extemporises drawing on a stock of 'riffs'. The point, as Toner points out (2001), is to evoke emotions associated with the country and totemic ancestors to which the songs pertain, and people associated with the country, especially the dead.

Songs accompany dances of three main kinds (Keen 1994). Women and girls dance in one spot, lifting their feet to the rhythm of the clapsticks while hand movements relate to the topic of the song. Men and boys dance in an arena in front of the singers, generally moving towards the singers in dance. In some ceremonies, including the *marradjirri* exchange ceremonies, of which the Marradjirri of the Djinang language group described by Borsboom is an example, the dances are peripatetic, movement through the camp representing the movement of protagonists in the related myth (e.g. a journey to the land of the dead in the Morning Star ceremony of the Djambar-rpuyngu group).

Singers learn several lengthy song-series belonging, in the case of men, to one's own patri-group (*ba:purru* or *mala*, 'clan') and one's mother's mother's group, as well as songs belonging to other closely related groups. Women have wider rights to sing mourning songs, including those of their mother's patri-group. The apparently formidable task of learning these songs is accomplished through long years of exposure to performances: at male initiation ceremonies (*dhapi*, 'foreskin'), mortuary ceremonies, and exchange ceremonies such as the Marradjirri. One will often observe a male singer with an infant boy cradled in his lap, while children sit or play near the women, who may dance on the spot, some way away from the singers, adjacent to an arena cleared for male dancers in front of the singers. Women encourage young children to dance and show them the appropriate hand movements. In the dance arena, boys and young men dance with the more expert adults, copying their movements: there is seldom a distinction between rehearsal and performance; novices learn by participating with the expert dancers.

When older men are present in the group of male singers, young men sing very quietly, playing clapsticks in unison, mumbling into their chests in deference to the older men. In certain contexts, however, it is evident that they have mastered the songs. One might hear a young man singing his *manikay* loudly while alone somewhere, perhaps in the motor workshop. One night at a funeral at Milingimbi at which I was present, the old men had retired, but the young men wanted to continue singing – they sang without the old men, perfectly confidently and competently, and loudly in contrast with their *sotto voce* performance earlier in the day. I have pointed out elsewhere (Keen 1994) that the Yolngu concept of knowledge implies the right to know: a young man or woman will claim not to be knowledgeable

71

where an older person or a person of another group has prior rights by virtue of age, patri-group identity or gender.

Learning in certain rituals contrasts strongly with regular exposure to *manikay* (and related dances) which are performed in public ceremonies, for they are performed less often. In initiation and revelatory rites, such as Nga:rra and Gunapipi, it is not just a matter of learning how to perform songs and dances and to make designs and objects. Part of the early experience of a Gunapipi ceremony, for young men at least, has more of the nature of an ordeal, for they are subject to dietary discipline, and must remain still and quiet for an extended period. In the Nga:rra, male novices are actively shown secret dances by first being faced away from the dances, then being turned to see them, after underarm sweat is applied to their eyes.

In the case of secret aspects of men's designs, teaching is rather formal (Morphy 1990). In fact, there is quite a lot of formal instruction in Yolngu society. I am thinking of the way in which adults point out to a child how particular individuals are related to them by kinship (*gurrutu*); as well as how a father will explain to a son, or an uncle to a nephew, the meaning of a design. The exegetical interpretations of songs and designs have to be formally imparted. (I am less knowledgeable about how young women learn about ritual matters.) The role of ritual expert (*djirrikaymirr, dalkarramirri*) requires memorising many sacred 'power names' associated with places belonging to many patri-groups especially of one's own patri-moiety. At a Nga: rra ceremony the *djirrikaymirr* must call out the appropriate names for many groups in turn, those of a particular group each day. Men insist on this ability as a key quality needed for the role.

How do Yolngu learning styles contrast with anthropological ones? The 'public' ceremonies consist primarily of long song-series, the language of which is somewhat esoteric, as well as mimetic dances. (The secret initiation and revelatory ceremonies are much more based on dance, especially the Nga:rra.) Apart from the informal aspects – the inter-personal interaction, disputes behind the scenes and so on – the only way for an anthropologist to gain something of the sense of songs and ceremonies is through transcription, translation and interviews, as well as unsolicited instruction. One must describe events as best one can in notebooks and, as Warner (1937) did some fifty years earlier, interview key participants on the basis of those notes, or sit with a key participant and transcribe songs or annotate film or videotape (e.g. Morphy 1984). This methodology can go against the grain of Yolngu interaction styles in which direct questions make people uncomfortable. I recall trying to record a Morning Star *marradjirri* ceremony at Milingimbi in 1975, carrying a reel-to-reel tape recorder, taking photographs, and trying to make notes all at the same time. I later asked a Djambarrpuyngu leader, the late Binyinyiwuy, what was the 'story' (*dhawu*) of the ceremony. He told me how people of one patri-group commissioned the ceremony by sending a gift of hair to the another group of a rather distant place, who performed it for the commissioning group, accompanied by the exchange of gifts. He did not offer to interpret the songs, or tell me the myth that relates to the ceremony. More in keeping with Yolngu learning styles, sometimes people take in upon themselves to teach a person aspects of their 'law' (*rom*), such as a body of designs and their meaning, or ritual relations between groups, or the nature of kin relatedness.

Anthropologists' reasons for learning about such matters usually involve 'learning that' more than 'learning how', and differ from those of Yolngu participants, who are concerned with 'learning how' as well as 'learning that'. For Yolngu it is a part of a way of life. For anthropologists it is a matter of contributing data, interpretations and explanations to the discipline as part of a broader explanatory enterprise, for example in the anthropology of religion, or of being a cultural broker and interpreter – a role which Ad Borsboom has performed so admirably.

References

Borsboom, A. 1978. *Maradjiri: A Modern Ritual Complex in Arnhem Land, North Australia* Nijmegen: Katholieke Universiteit Nijmegen, PhD thesis.

Christie, M. J. 1984. *The Classroom World of the Aboriginal Child* Brisbane, University of Queensland, PhD thesis,

Hamby, L. 2001. *Containers of Power: Fibre Forms from Northeast Arnhem Land, Australia* Canberra, Australian National University, PhD thesis.

Harris, S. 1984. *Culture and Learning: Tradition and Education in Northeast Arnhem Land* Canberra: Australian Institute of Aboriginal Studies.

Keen, I. 1994. *Knowledge and Secrecy in an Aboriginal Religion: Yolngu of Northeast Arnhem Land* Oxford: Clarendon Press.

Morphy, H. 1984. *Journey to the Crocodile's Nest: An Accompanying Monograph to the Film Madarrpa Funeral at Gurka'wuy by Ian Dunlop* Canberra: Australian Institute of Aboriginal Studies.

Morphy, H. 1990. *Ancestral Connections: Art and an Aboriginal System of Knowledge* Chicago, University of Chicago Press.

Toner, P. 2001. *When the Echoes Are Gone: A Yolngu Musical Anthropology* Canberra, Australian National University, PhD thesis.

Warner, W.L. 1937. *A Black Civilisation: A Social Study of an Australian Tribe* New York, Harper.

Learning to Be White
in Guadeloupe

Janine Klungel

Throughout my fieldwork in Guadeloupe, I was repeatedly confronted with the ways in which black Guadeloupians commented on my whiteness. From the very outset, I was habitually identified as '*la blanche*' (the white woman), but in the eyes of many I continued to fall short of the normative rules of white conduct. Children would be the most severe judges of my whiteness, whenever they glanced at my hair and listened to my French, only to conclude their assessment by shaking their heads disapprovingly. Due to their critical remarks, I became acutely aware of the social construction of dominant white-ness in Guadeloupe – a Caribbean island that was colonised by France in 1635, where Africans were enslaved until 1848, and that has remained an overseas territory of France to this day.

Whiteness is not primarily a visual mark says Judith Butler (1993), but an act that needs to be performed to sustain that position. The Martinican psychiatrist of colonial oppression Frantz Fanon dilated upon this topic already in *Peau noire, masques blancs* (1952). In analysing the symbolic violence caused by the forceful instigation of whiteness in the French Antilles, he focussed on the conduct of black Antilleans who had migrated to France and returned to the island as whites. They greeted others with nods, spoke French with rolling r's, wore French fashion, and behaved superior.[18] I was frequently punished for not displaying these excellent qualities of whiteness. In the following five lessons, I will describe how Guadeloupians drew atten-tion to my anomalous whiteness and taught me to be white.

Lesson 1: Once I went on a daytrip to the Steps of the Slaves in Petit-Canal that was organised by a women's association. I was welcomed by the president, who incited the crowd to applaud for the

---

[18] Presently, black Guadeloupeans who behave as whites are called 'Bounties', especially by Africans. This is a reference to the well-known chocolate bar with a coconut filling: black on the outside, white on the inside.

anthropologist from the Netherlands. When I decided to help the organisation preparing food and distributing the cake, I transgressed the code of white conduct and was punished for it by a light-skinned lady. She cast a deadly glance at me and yelled angrily that I had to hurry up and serve her first, whereupon she snatched the piece of cake out of my hands. To the woman sitting next to her, she bluntly remarked: 'if she acts like a *nègre*, I will treat her that way.' The woman did not like that I started serving, for it is considered inappropriate white behaviour. White people let themselves be served.

Lesson 2: Homeless people in particular taught me how to behave properly as a white woman. Ceaselessly scouring the streets of Guadeloupe's most central town Pointe-à-Pitre, they would greet me from afar, 'Snow white, you must have a lot of coins in your pocket!' Pierre, a tall, skinny drug addict always used to pop up whenever I took a step outside and accompanied me on my walks through the city. We enjoyed each other's company, because to a certain degree we were both socially incongruent. On one occasion, Pierre happened to see from a distance how I took out my purse in public. He immediately came running towards me and scolded me for not making his task of protecting me, *une blanche*, very easy. He constantly drummed it into me that as a white woman I had to distrust everybody and be careful, otherwise I would be an all-too-easy target for robbers. I learned from Pierre that white people do not trust anybody.

Lesson 3: In my contact with Caroline, a tall homeless androgynous Haitian woman who was also addicted to crack, I was painfully reminded of Pierre's warnings. Sometimes she would invite me to smoke a cigarette with her. We did not share a common language, but I liked to be around her and tried to help by buying her food and boxes of sanitary towels. When I met her anew in the *Saint Pierre and Saint Paul* cathedral after one year of absence, she was in dire need of a dose and ordered me to give her money. I gave her some, but she became furious, and commanded me to hand her my purse, 'or *Blan* I will break your skull.' I got out of the pew and sought shelter close to an old lady, who yelled at her and subsequently began to reprimand me: 'how stupid can you be!' She was annoyed, because as a white woman I had to know that I should always be chaperoned.

Lesson 4: Fijah, a long Rasta man with an enormous turban of dreadlocks, taught me a similar lesson. As I passed him by, carrying two bulky shopping bags while sweat was pouring off my face and body – not a very ladylike nor white performance to begin with – he looked over his sunglasses and cast me a look of derision and said: 'you know, I have often asked myself if I would pick up *la blanche* if you fell in the street, because you never say hello to me.' 'Well,' I answered, 'then I do not hope to fall in front of you. I usually say hello to you, but you never return my greeting, so I thought that you did not appreciate it.' 'Where are you from?' he asked. 'The Netherlands', I replied. 'You see, I could immediately tell that you are not a French lady; otherwise you would never have talked to me.' Fijah taught me that white people avoid black persons; they definitely do not greet and talk to them.

Lesson 5: Meanwhile, I stayed with an extended African-Guadeloupian family – the Sangely – who live together in a yard in the countryside of Guadeloupe. My white conduct was also closely monitored in this context. Isabelle, the matrifocal pivot of the Sangely, made sure that I adhered to the rules of white conduct as defined by the medical hot-cold syndrome. White persons, who are perceived as cold, should never come into contact with hotness too abruptly, because it causes an imbalance in their bodies and brings about disease. With saintly patience, Isabelle taught me how to protect myself against hotness. If I was venturing outside in the blazing sunshine, she ran after me with a straw head. If I was about to sink my teeth into a piece of fruit categorized as hot, she made sure that I only ate it when my body had already been warmed up. Upon leaving Guadeloupe, I understood how my incorrect white conduct had been a constant source of anxiety to Isabelle, because I had unwittingly brought myself on the verge of illness or worse on many occasions. She told me: 'I did not want to be the person to inform your parents about your death.'

In methodological handbooks on ethnographic research, anthropologists are taught that the success of their research is largely determined by the ability to establish good rapport. I have to acknowledge that my whiteness by itself prevented me from doing so numerous times. My improper white conduct only worsened the situation, because it irritated black Guadeloupians that I did not act like a proper white person. Why was I so stupid to jeopardize the privileges attached to whiteness in Guadeloupian society? For what reasons had I come to Guadeloupe anyway? 'Did you come to bring us development?' some people asked me cynically. I always found it difficult to answer this question, since my reply 'to do anthropological research' always sounded weak. Although anthropologists are taught that they have to participate as much as possible in the daily activities of the people among and with whom they do their research, as well as to attempt to learn, as far as possible, to think, see, feel, and act like them by participating in their lives, I was frequently laughed at when I described the art of fieldwork to black Guadeloupians. They found it ridiculous that a white woman had come, on her own, all the way from the Netherlands to learn from them.

In contrast, I was not particularly eager to learn to be white in accordance with French colonial rules of white conduct. Therefore, the many critical comments I received from black Guadeloupians concerning my poor performance of whiteness, oftentimes made me feel ill at ease and frustrated me, because I was only allowed to immerse myself in their lives if I adopted my designated role and accepted my place in the local colour hierarchy. However, the advantage of my anomalous whiteness was that I often found myself transgressing implicit rules, which in turn gave me a privileged position to learn about the dominant scheme of whiteness in Guadeloupian society (cf. Douglas 1966). Before I finish, I am curious to know, if you, Ad, have had similar experiences during your fieldwork. What was it like for you to be a *white fella* in Australia?

REFERENCES

Butler, J. 1993. *Bodies That Matter: On the Discursive Limits of 'Sex'* New York, Routledge.
Douglas, M. 1966. *Purity and Danger* London, Kegan Paul.
Fanon, F. 1952. *Peau noire, masques blancs* Paris, Éditions de Seuil.

Learning from 'the Other', Writing about 'the Other'

Jean Kommers

Once, when writing down field notes in a Kipsigis compound, some-thing happened which struck me deeply. A small, four-year-old boy, accompanied by his mother, entered the compound. Seeing me, the boy asked his mother: 'What is that man doing here? He is just sitting, writing and reading, but he doesn't know anything about the compound: he doesn't know how to care for the goats and the cows, and he knows nothing about the maize! What is his use?' The mother hastened to silence the boy, but in vain: the message was clear.

Of course, as a fieldwork experience, the incident was far from unique: most anthropologists will recognize the lesson in modesty. In ethnography, the theme even has become a *topos*. Perhaps anthro-pology is anomalous among social sciences in that within our disci-pline a tradition of reflection on the 'ignorant researcher' (Borsboom 1996: 104) has developed.

To me the incident was one out of many comparable experiences, but this time it was special. As became clear afterwards, in this case people felt truly embarrassed. Indeed, the guest ought to be treated with respect and according to his (high) age as a wise and knowing man. The same evening the boy's older brother was sent over to commence my education on how to feed the cows, how to recognize individual goats and how to evaluate the condition of the maize. The situation was awkward from the start, especially for my young tutor: a young boy instructing an old man, using teaching-methods akin to those which he knew from primary school and which he thought adequate in relation to a stranger. The venture did not last long and no grown-ups interfered. But it made me reflect on a theme that has become fashionable in certain circles: 'learning from the Other'.

Particularly in cases where there is a direct confrontation of conflicting epistemologies, 'learning from the Other' and the transmission of the acquired knowledge may pose special problems: in such instances the problem of anthropological representation 'meets its greatest test' (Stoller 1989: 39). In many projects that imply bringing closely together representatives of totally different epistemological traditions, ranging from micro-finance projects to interventions into the position of indigenous healers, these problems are particularly pressing and difficult to discuss. Therefore, attempts to make anthropological representations concerning such subjects accessible to the general public deserve our special interest.

Ad's *De clan van de Wilde Honing* may be considered an important starting point for a reflection on this theme. The book not only describes how the fieldworker 'learns' nor merely underscores the importance of 'learning from the Other', but also informs its readers about 'exotic' forms of transmitting knowledge. Besides, Ad produced a particular kind of text – the 'popular' account – that is aimed at the general public. His book is an admirable attempt resulting in a text in which the author's own position of authoritative informer – derived from conventional, recognizable and acceptable ways of identifying and transmitting knowledge – is at stake, but readers are also constantly confronted with their epistemological presuppositions.

To learn 'from the people' is a popular dictum in treatises on participant observation. It is closely related to a specific genre in ethnography: the so-called *confessional tales* (Van Maanen 1988: 75). Even in the development industry the theme seems to gain importance. Instead of the paternalistic 'outsider's views', which resulted in so many failing projects, small-scale projects undeniably seem to imply a certain measure of openness towards the idea of 'learning from the Other' (Huizer 1992). Mostly, however, the idea concerns 'practical learning', for instance the acknowledgement in agricultural projects that other peoples up to a certain degree 'know their environment' (compare e.g. Mortimore 1998). The tangible character of such phenomena may tempt students to undervalue epistemological problems involved in the transmission of knowledge. Only on rare occasions does the idea of 'learning from the other' comprise reflections about the social position of the person who wants to learn (Borsboom 2006); about changing attitudes of Western scientists regarding indigenous knowledge systems (Slikkerveer 1989), about other epistemologies (Hoppers 2002), about the interdependence between 'our' knowledge and 'theirs' (Hobart 1993), and about forms and methods of teaching characteristic for the culture(s) under consideration (Ndegwah 2007). To be sure: numerous publications exist on each of these topics; reflections comprising a combination of these various domains, however, are rare, particularly in the sphere of 'application'. Thus, in a recent periodical for medical students, experiences with 'traditional healers' could be described in pejorative phrasings, without generating the slightest embarrassment among the editors (*Radbode* October 2007). It seems that Slikkerveer's conclusion still holds: 'the negative values and attitudes of the evolutionists have persisted into our days' (1989: 130). Thus, notwithstanding the impressive testimonies given by e.g. Basil Davidson regarding the ingenuity and creativity of African knowledge systems, to many people who try to 'develop' Africa, the continent 'still' suffers from inadequate and defective knowledge systems. Only on rare occasions does one seem to be aware that one's own ideas about the Other suffer greatly from a lack of insight into other knowledge systems or from inadequate methods to analyze these systems. Anthropologists are well acquainted with this problem, however it still seems very difficult to extend the message to other disciplines. To transmit knowledge about 'exotic' ways of knowledge-transmission and knowledge-production to a public not used to reflection about ethnocentrisms and ignorant about the (history of its) own epistemology, appears to be very difficult. That is why Ad's attempt to describe Aboriginal knowledge in the context of the 'spiritual wealth' of Australian Aboriginal culture in a way that is accessible to a general public is so important. It proved to be a 'long seller': first published in 1996, the Dutch version has seen several editions, the most recent one dated 2007. For a small linguistic area, this may be an indication of exceptional success.

Amongst professionals, however, these types of 'popularizing' texts often arouse mixed feelings, while they tend to stress the problematic aspects: inevitably these writings simplify complex social and cultural realities; they usually undervalue the methodological intricacies behind representations, and the 'popular' language implied by the genre may be inadequate to express the other world (Van Maanen

1988: 24-25). Often, too, authors of popular treatises have to make use of a variety of generic forms which lend their writings an experimental character easily to be misunderstood by specific categories of readers. They have to oscillate between very different narratives and narrative forms (Borsboom 1996: 97), while using a language familiar to their readers. This proves to be a particularly delicate enterprise when subjects are concerned about which the author *and* reader both 'know' that the Other is wrong. In anthropology, a classic case is David Livingstone's dialogue with the rain-maker (Livingstone 1857: 23-25).

Ad's *De clan van de Wilde Honing* offers a nice counter example when describing Aboriginal treatment of illness (1996: 160-171). Here I will not venture to deconstruct the text, but will confine my comments to some cursory remarks. Ad introduces the theme by referring to what happened one time when he fell ill. According to some friends, he should consult an Aboriginal healer. But he had his doubts, as he confesses to the reader: he would not be able to pretend to believe in a treatment during which the healer would 'mutter inexplicable words', while performing 'all sorts of' actions followed by 'conjuring up' an object out of his body. 'Should I feign that with this my complaint has disappeared?' (1996: 160)

In an admirable fashion, Ad tries to explain the position and significance of indigenous healers, concluding his discussion with the statement that the extraction of an object from the body of the diseased 'confronts any western observer with a problem.' As he writes: 'On the one hand one impossibly can accept that such an object really was in the body of the diseased. On the other hand, the indigenous belief in this is so strong, that without such a trick many healings wouldn't take place' (1996: 170). To clarify this aspect to the reader, Ad starts by posing a rhetoric question: 'Is the healer also a clever illusionist?' The answer is: the healer 'knows' that he is manipulating material objects in an accomplished way, but these objects demonstrate 'in fact' what is happening on the spiritual level.

This interpretation may evoke serious questions about observation, epistemology and representation. In this case, observation and argument did not transcend the author's epistemological framework and remained embedded in a logic familiar not only to the author but also to the reader, resulting in a representation built on 'common sense' expressions. Of course the rhetorical 'trick' is that the author identifies with the reader, anticipating his or her prejudices (even underscoring these by expressing his own doubts), followed by an explanation in which action and object (until now prominent in the discussion) are made subordinate to person and (indigenous) inter-pretation (compare Fraser 1990).

To paraphrase Paul Stoller, in such cases only 'epistemological humility' fits the stranger (Stoller 1989: 5, compare especially 121: 'To hear or not to hear') and 'learning from the Other' becomes a matter of 'redefining our orientation to sight [and hearing]' to quit the 'scientific gaze' (9, 43). This may be sound advice to professional anthropologists, but could it be applicable in the transmission of 'exotic' knowledge to outsiders? In his book Ad succeeded in a remarkable way to reach aims implied by this advice. However, as this case about indigenous healing may illustrate, in particular subjects involving different and seemingly mutually exclusive epistemologies, discussions bearing upon the transmission of knowledge about ('exotic') knowledge, pose great problems, even to the most able and experienced anthropologist. Attempts to discuss such subjects in a way accessible to the general public become more and more pressing, however, in a world in which paternalistic ways of knowledge trans-mission are incompatible with attitudes and policies changing in favour of the emancipation of local ('indigenous') knowledge systems (Hoppers 2002). To this discussion Ad's book is a most valuable contribution. His way of representing the world of the Aborigines highly inspires reflection about this important and topical issue.

References

Borsboom, A. 1996. *De clan van de Wilde Honing: Spirituele rijkdom van de Aborigines* Haarlem, Becht.
Fraser, R. ed. 1990. *Sir James Frazer and the Literary Imagination: Essays in Affinity and Influence* London, MacMillan
Huizer, G. 1992. *Leren van de Derde Wereld: Crisis als uitdaging* Kampen, Kok Agora.
Hobart, M. 1993. *An Anthropological Critique of Development: The Growth of Ignorance* London, Routledge.
Hoppers, C. ed. 2002. *Indigenous Knowledge and the Integration of Knowledge Systems* Claremont, New Africa Education.

Livingstone, D. 1857. *Missionary Travels and Researches in South Africa* London, John Murray.

Mortimore, M. 1998. *Roots in the African Dust: Sustaining the Drylands* Cambridge: Cambridge University Press.

Ndegwah, D. 2007. *Biblical Hermeneutics as a Tool for Inculturation in Africa* Nairobi, Kijabe Printing Press.

Slikkerveer, L.J. 1989. 'Changing Values and Attitudes of Social and Natural Scientists towards Indigenous Peoples and their Knowledge Systems' eds. D.M. Warren, L. J. Slikkerveer and S. O. Titilola *Indigenous Knowledge Systems: Implications for Agriculture and International Development* Ames, Iowa State University: 121-137.

Stoller, P. 1989. *The Taste of Ethnographic Things: The Senses in Anthropology* Philadelphia, University of Pennsylvania Press.

Van Maanen, John 1988. *Tales from the Field. On Writing Ethnography.* Chicago and London, University of Chicago Press.

Maori Styles of Teaching and Learning

Toon van Meijl

My education as a Maori was a matter of observation while I grew up in this complete community. It was a community where children were allowed to do their thing, where there was a place for the aged, and a place for the middle-aged. These places were within the structure of tribal organisation. I had to move through this as an apprenticeship for group living. We had to learn the dynamics of group living. We had to learn how to live together because we were in one another's pockets. If we didn't, problems would have arisen. From the time we were children we had to learn what it meant to be part of an extended family. We were warned not to do some things and we learned by others' experience.

John Rangihau (1975: 165)

New Zealand is often contrasted with Australia as a country with more exemplary relations between its indigenous population, the Maori, and the European settler majority. Although Maori social and economic indicators are comparatively more favourable, however, the indigenous people continue to lag behind the average European New Zealander. The latest census figures dating from 2006 have reconfirmed the gap between Maori and non-Maori (or Pakeha, as they are generally labelled in New Zealand). Disparities between Maori and Pakeha are evident in most dimensions of society, including education.

The latest statistics show that the gap in secondary and tertiary educational achievement for Maori versus non-Maori is still significant. Maori school retention rates have recently improved, but Maori are still leaving school earlier than Pakeha. In addition, almost 40 per cent of Maori have no formal qualification as against 25 per cent of non-Maori. Furthermore, Maori continue to lag in post-school qualifications with about 28 per cent of Maori holding one, compared with almost 40 per cent of Pakeha. Thus, disparities between Maori and non-Maori remain, in spite of Maori improvements over the past few decades.

A variety of reasons has been advanced to explain the undesirable discrepancies in education between Maori and Pakeha. Some argue that socio-economic differences between the two population groups outweigh all other factors, but it is more often contended that cultural differences play a decisive role. Indeed, it is generally claimed that there is a mismatch between the New Zealand education system and the cultural circumstances in which Maori children are raised. In this debate it is always assumed that the cultural principles underlying Maori educational practices are completely different from European understandings of education. Attempts to draw out Maori principles of education are, however, few and far between (e.g. Metge 1984). In this paper I will therefore endeavour to present a preliminary outline of the cultural strategies, practices and principles of teaching and learning in Maori society.

Strategies

Western educational theories make a clear-cut distinction between teaching and learning, and between teacher and learner, which is reflected in different concepts. The Maori language, however, uses only one word, *ako*, meaning both 'to teach' and 'to learn '. This is converted into a noun meaning 'teacher' (*kai-ako*) by a prefix indicating actor, and into one meaning 'learner' (*akonga*) by adding a noun ending (Pere 1982). Thus, verbally the Maori approach emphasizes the unified cooperation of teacher and learner in a single enterprise, which is also expressed in Maori education strategies.

In carrying out the task of educating the rising generation of young Maori in Maori ways, Maori have used three major strategies over the last 25 years. First, there is the formal 'house of learning' or *whare waananga*, which currently comprises several fairly distinct types. The *whare waananga* can be a formal school in which a few experts instruct a small number of selected students in certain branches of sacred knowledge, mainly by the method of rote learning. Furthermore, the concept of *whare waananga* is used in reference to a college of acknowledged experts, who share and debate the knowledge they hold individually with the aim of establishing the 'truth', often embodied in an authorised version. Finally, the term is also applied to any gathering where Maori come together to share knowledge and debate issues, traditional as well as modern.

The second educational strategy used by Maori is, in contrast to the formal *whare waananga*, informal and more embedded in the ongoing life of the community. It could be called education through exposure. Prospective learners are found, drawn or thrown into situations in which their participation is needed and expected, given some help by the others involved to develop the skills needed and to make sense of what is going on but left to a large degree to 'pick it up' and 'work it out' by themselves. The emphasis is on letting things happen naturally, and taking advantage of them when and as they do. All children learn a great deal this way, especially in the early years.

Between the two strategies of exposure and *whare waananga* there is a third, which I shall tentatively call the apprenticeship or tutorial strategy. This occurs when a wise older person takes a selected pupil under his or her wing and 'feeds' him or her with assorted kinds of knowledge. The pupil may be taken as a baby, a child or adult. The intimate association may last a short period or for years. The 'apprentice' is usually but not always a kinsman and may or may not be the only one in training at a time. The most common example occurs when a grandparent or grandparents take a *mokopuna* ('grandchild') to live with them from birth. This *moko taura* is attached to the grandparents as a 'rope' and may be considered as the lifeline linking the old people to their descendants.

Practices

In practice the three Maori educational strategies are not mutually exclusive, but they occur in varying combinations, as when a grandfather takes his grandchild everywhere as a constant companion, visiting kin, attending ceremonial gatherings, even when old enough to the *whare waananga*. Separately and together the three strategies involve practices and approaches which, in turn, suggest certain underlying principles and assumptions.

A distinctive feature of Maori educational practices is that there is no formal teacher training. Elderly people are free to pass on their knowledge when and how they please. Almost everybody is a 'teacher' at some stage and to some extent. 'Teaching' is a fairly unspecialised role. As a result, 'teaching' varies considerably in effectiveness, in the methods used, and in the degree to which 'teachers' borrow from or react against the teacher model provided by the school system. However, certain styles of teaching emerge so frequently that it would seem fair to see them as characteristically Maori.

Thus, in Maori teaching practices a marked emphasis is usually placed on the learner looking, listening and imitating, with a minimum of words, whether of instruction or discussion. This is particularly strong in the early stage of learning, whether with children or adult learners. Parents, grandparents and other instructors often say *'Haere mai, whakarongo mai, titiro mai. Me peenei.'* ('Come here, listen, look. Like this.'). Learners are often directed to sit or stand alongside the 'teacher'.

Alternatively, it could be argued that Maori teaching is not a matter of 'practising what you preach' so much as 'preaching by your practice'. It is primarily teaching by demonstration. Moreover, this applies not only to practical skills, but also to basic values, such as respect, hospitality, and *aroha* ('love') to kin and those less fortunate than oneself. Whatever people do, there is always a teaching point in it. This approach of teaching also implies that learners are encouraged to learn not only by doing but by doing tasks in their proper setting. For that reason, too, learning in groups is favoured over the individual working on his or her own, while the most important learning processes probably take place in peer groups.

Principles

It seems to me that Maori teaching practices are not a random assortment, but hang together in a coherent pattern which points to the existence of a set of related principles, an underlying understanding of education. Many Maori engaged in the task of education take these principles for granted, but since they are only marginally recognized in New Zealand it is inevitable to make them more explicit.

First, in Maori thinking knowledge is precious: it is a *taonga* or 'treasure' to be cherished. It has *mana* or 'spiritual power [or] prestige' while it also may confer *mana*. It should be coveted and aspired to, but not too easily attained. Therefore, it should be protected with barriers tough enough to test the commitment and perseverance of its seekers.

Knowledge is of different kinds. It can be classified in several ways. An important distinction is made between those aspects of knowledge which are regarded as *tapu* ('restricted'), because of closeness to the spiritual dimension, and those which are not. The translation of *tapu* as 'restricted', by the way, does not so much concern the knowledge itself or the right to hear it which is guarded, than the right to use and discuss it in public as an authority. After all, for Maori the ultimate aim of knowing is understanding, *maatau*, the grasp of inner meaning, knowing things in their essence and in their patterns.

The concept of *maatau*, in turn, is linked to the main principle of Maori education which involves that it is essentially continuing education, an ongoing lifelong process passing through a set of stages. A learner must learn certain things, show signs of mastery before being allowed to progress further. Learning depends on readiness, both actual and as assessed by the 'teacher'. There are some things some people are never ready for. On the whole, children are expected to be concerned with exploring and developing the senses rather than the intellect. In the past, adults even actively discouraged children and even young people from showing what they considered a premature interest in subjects that required maturity. 'Wait till you are older, then you'll understand' is a common saying in Maori society.

Finally, the Maori view of education as of life emphasizes wholeness and connectedness. It eschews compartmentalisation. It puts together things that Western thinking separates, characteristically tackles several subjects at once and pursues several goals. It aims at nothing less than comprehensive education.

Conclusion

The contrast between the Maori way of education and the European are self-evident, although naturally they also have many things in common. Nevertheless, it is important to point out that Maori children raised by adults operating on a different set of premises are disadvantaged in the New Zealand school system, or that their strengths are not recognised because not expected. In addition, the social and economic changes that have taken place in New Zealand over the last fifty years put the Maori way, developed under different circumstances, increasingly under pressure and adversely affected its currency and effectiveness. These problems are generally tackled by insisting that Maori make all the accommodations, but the situation could also be changed by accommodating the dominant education system in New Zealand to the Maori style of teaching and learning, which contains insights that are indeed of wider relevance.

REFERENCES

Metge, J. 1984. *Learning and Teaching: He Tikanga Maori* Wellington, Department of Education, Maori and Island Division.
Pere, R.R. 1982. *Ako: Concepts and Learning in the Maori Tradition* Hamilton, University of Waikato, Department of Sociology, Working Paper No. 17.
Rangihau, J. 1975. 'Being Maori' ed. M. King *Te Ao Hurihuri: The World Moves On* Auckland, Longman Paul: 165-175.

Tutorials as Integration into a Study Environment

Ariana Need

In the course 'Theory Construction: Anthropologists and Sociologists on Religion', two lectures were dedicated to the work of Emile Durkheim. More specifically, the focus was on his work *The Elementary Forms of Religious Life*, first published in French in 1912 as *Les formes élémentaires de la vie religieuse: Le système totémique en Australie*.[19] Ad Borsboom devoted one lecture to the totemic principle; in the second lecture I focused on the sociological aspects of Durkheim's work. My lecture started with Durkheim's definition of religion as 'a unified system of beliefs and practices [...] which unite into one single moral community'[20], to ultimately arrive at the conclusion that the true purpose of religion is social. Religion serves as the carrier of social sentiments, and, most importantly, offers rituals that tie individuals to their community.[21]

In the closing discussion, I habitually confronted the students with Durkheim's remark that in his day and age the old gods were growing old or had already dead, while others had not yet been born.[22] I questioned my students about what new gods might have been born and what new religion might have emerged since Durkheim published his book. Furthermore, I quizzed them on what this new religion would consider sacred and which rituals would be part of this religion. Almost every single year, there was at least one student who answered that the new religion might be based on the sanctity of knowledge, with universities serving as places of worship and in which tutorials could be viewed as the most important rituals. In this contribution, I will proceed from the idea that rituals create bonds

---

[19] E. Durkheim. 1995 [1912]. *The Elementary Forms of Religious Life* New York, The Free Press.

[20] E. Durkheim. *The Elementary Forms of Religious Life*: 44.

[21] D.L. Pals. 1996. *Seven Theories of Religion* Oxford: Oxford University Press: 111.

[22] E. Durkheim. *The Elementary Forms of Religious Life*: 429.

between individuals and their social group, and that during rituals the norms of the group are imprinted in the minds of the individuals. I will do this by examining the academic consequences of participation of students in 'college-rituals', the tutorial.

In *Leaving College: Rethinking the Causes and Cures of Student Attrition*, Vincent Tinto offers a theory that explains student attrition from institutions of higher education.[23] Building on the work of Van Gennep and Durkheim, a central element of his theory is the concept of social integration. It emphasizes the experiences and processes of integration and their impact on student retention and college persistence. The so-called Amsterdam model of educational careers combines insights from Tinto's work with economic theories.[24] It conceives of educational careers as longitudinal processes, which contain the sequence of prior influences – goals – assessment of attainability of goals – commitments – experiences – *integration* – adjustment of goals – adjustment of assessment of attainability of goals.

Need and De Jong examined one cycle of this longitudinal process, and concluded that local study environments only have minor influences on the academic success of Dutch college students. Most differences in the academic success of students can be attributed to differences between individual students, and these differences do not systematically correlate with characteristics of the local study environment.[25] However, in the study by Need and De Jong the process of academic integration is not directly measured; the outcome of this process in terms of academic achievement is used to indicate how well students are integrated in their local study environments. In this contribution, I consider attendance of tutorials as a more direct indicator of study integration, and consider to what extent it is related with students' achievements. For this purpose, I use the *Student Monitor 2002*, a representative survey of students in Dutch Higher

---

[23] V. Tinto. 1993. *Leaving College: Rethinking the Causes and Cures of Student Attrition* Chicago: University of Chicago Press, 2nd edition.

[24] U. de Jong, J. Roeleveld and D. Webbink. 1997. *Studeren in de jaren negentig: Verder studeren: Eindrapport* Den Haag: Ministerie van Onderwijs, Cultuur en Wetenschap.

[25] A. Need and U. de Jong. 2001. 'Do Local Study Environments Matter? A Multilevel Analysis of the Educational Careers of First-Year College Students' *Higher Education in Europe* 26: 263-278.

Education in 2002.[26] In the ensuing analyses, I examine to what extent tutorials affect the academic achievements of students, thereby serving as integrating rituals tying the students to their local study environments. To assess the effect of student participation in tutorials properly and proportionally, it is necessary to take into account the effect of other factors. In this analysis, I therefore control for the effects of sex, level of study, prior achievements, the number of hours students spend attending lectures and the number of hours students study by themselves.

Analysis

In the *Student Monitor* 2002, students from all institutions of higher education answered various questions relating to their studies. For the present analysis, I selected students who were not in the last year of their studies – since these students tend to devote a lot of time to writing their theses. Secondly, I selected students from the social sciences. These students mostly resemble the anthropologists and sociologists who took the course 'Theory Construction: Anthropologists and Sociologists on Religion'. And finally, students were removed from the analysis if they did not provide complete information on all questions in the survey that are relevant to the analysis. Due to these selection criteria, 404 students were left for the analysis. Table 1 describes the students in the sample.

The achievements of the students – the central dependent variable in the analysis – is constructed on the basis of the answers students gave to the question what percentage of last year's courses they successfully completed. This variable ranges between 0 and 100. Table 1 shows that on average students have completed 62.3 per cent of the courses in the past year. Attending tutorials is the least common form of learning that is distinguished here. Ranging between 0 and 40 hours a week, we see that the average social science student spends less than 4 hours a week (3.7) attending tutorials. On average, the students in the sample spend 7 hours a week attending lectures; this

---

[26] A. Hofman, J. de Boom, E. Heyl, U. de Jong, M. van Leeuwen and I. van der Veen. 2003. *Studentenmonitor 2002: Kernrapport* Den Haag: Ministerie van Onderwijs, Cultuur en Wetenschap.

Table 1: Describing the students in social sciences in the sample of the *Student Monitor 2002* (N=404)

	Average	Minimum score	Maximum score
Achievements (% of courses this year)	62.3	0	100
Tutorials (hours a week)	3.7	0	40
Lectures (hours a week)	7.0	0	30
Self-study (hours a week)	11.9	0	40
Women	0.71	0	1
University	0.64	0	1
Prior achievements: Average exam score high school	6.8	5.8	8.6

Source: *Student Monitor 2002*; own calculations

varies between 0 hours and 30 hours a week. Self-study ranges between 0 and 40 hours a week, and has an average score of 11.9.

Table 1 also provides information about the background of the social science students in 2002. First, and this is not surprising given the selection of students in the social sciences, we see that the vast majority of the students (71 per cent) is female. Secondly, in this selection, 64 per cent of the students study at university; the remaining students (36 per cent) attend a form of higher vocational education. On average, the exam score in higher education of the students in our sample is 6.8. This exam score varies between 5.8 and 8.6.[27]

To formally test to what extent tutorials affect the academic achievements of students, we performed a regression analysis using the percentage of courses students completed in the past year as the dependent variable. I simultaneously estimated the effect of the number of hours students spend attending lectures, the number of hours students study by themselves, sex, level of study, and prior achievements. We have subtracted the average score from the average high school exam score, the weekly number of hours spend on tutorials, the weekly number of hours spend attending lectures, and the

---

[27] In some cases, attending lectures will be a precondition for successfully completing a course. Unfortunately, the survey did not ask the students to report on their grades, which would have been a better measure for academic achievement than the one I use in this contribution.

weekly number of hours used for self-study. This makes the results in Table 2 more straightforward to interpret. Table 2 shows the results of this regression analysis. It presents unstandardized coefficients, their standard errors and the significance of the effects.

Table 2: Analysing the effect of attending tutorials on academic achievements (regression analysis; N=404)

	Unstandardized Coefficients	Std. Error	Sig.
Constant	63.60	3.32	0.00
Tutorials (hours a week)	1.52	0.29	0.00
Lectures (hours a week)	-0.17	0.27	0.53
Self-study (hours a week)	0.51	0.17	0.00
Women	5.92	3.05	0.05
University	-8.70	2.98	0.00
Prior achievements: Average exam score high school	1.65	2.68	0.54

Source: *Student Monitor 2002*; own calculations

The constant in Table 2 refers to the estimated percentage of courses completed for a student with a score of 0 for all other variables in the model. Thus, the constant refers to a male student in higher vocational education, who takes 3.7 hours of tutorials – the average –, who on a weekly basis spends 7 hours attending lectures and 11.9 hours of self-study, and who had an exam score of 6.8 in high school. The estimated percentage of courses completed for this student is 63.6.

The unstandardized coefficient of taking tutorials is 1.52. This indicates that if students spend one hour extra at tutorials, the percentage of courses they complete in a year would be 1.52 higher. This effect is significant. There is no significant direct effect found of the number of weekly hours spend at taking lectures. Self-study, on the other hand, does have a significant effect on college achievements, although it is smaller than that of taking tutorials. Table 2 also shows that women tend to complete more courses per year than men, and that students at university complete less courses per year than students of vocational education. Finally, students who performed well at their exams in high school, tend to complete more courses than students who obtained lower exam scores.

Summing Up the Evidence

In this contribution, I tested the Durkheimian hypothesis that attending rituals in educational institutions increases students' academic achievements. Just like attending rituals in church increases the chances that individuals will live up to the teachings of the church, it is assumed that attending tutorials increases the likelihood that students will remember what a tutor is trying to teach them. The results of the analysis presented in this contribution are clear: whereas attending lectures has no effect on the percentage of courses that students complete, attending tutorials does. One hour extra per week attending tutorials increases the yearly percentage of courses that is completed with one and an half per cent. Based on these results, perhaps the best advise to institutes of higher education would be that increasing the number of tutorials – and accompanying these with home assignments – might be a good way to increase the academic success of their students.

The Transmission
of Kinship Knowledge

Catrien Notermans

In Dutch society, it is generally assumed that children have to grow up with their birth parents in order for them to develop into well-balanced adult people. In contrast, Cameroonian parents are supposed to respect the rule that children cannot stay with them all the time, for the latter must be granted the opportunity to live with different kin members. Parents who keep their children at their side are accused of being selfish and antisocial, as they prevent close kin members from sharing in their upbringing. Such children are sincerely pitied because they are isolated from their extended kin network and thereby jeopardised considerably in a context of ever-changing household compositions. From babyhood onwards, children learn not to become attached solely to their birth parents but to see different aunts and uncles as their 'mothers' and 'fathers'. This essay explores how kinship knowledge – in particular, knowledge about which kin can be seen as reliable parents – is transmitted from parents to children. What are the ideological and practical reasons for plural parenthood? How do children get used to it? And how easy is it, for both parents and children, to follow the kinship rules? But first, I will briefly introduce the Cameroonian setting on which this ethnographic essay is based.

Batouri is a small provincial town with 25,000 inhabitants in the savannah area in East Cameroon, 500 kilometres from the capital Yaoundé. One part of town, called Mbondossi, is inhabited by approximately 1,500 people who have their ethnic origin in Batouri or its surrounding villages. Social life in Mbondossi is characterized by practices of matrilineal descent, high frequency of polygyny, high marital flexibility, and high numbers of temporarily fostered children (children not living with their biological mother). One out of three children lives with foster parents, and school surveys show even higher percentages: 49% of primary schoolchildren between 9 and 15 years old and 94% of secondary schoolchildren between 13 and 18 years old live with foster parents. Even children who actually stay with their first parents have usually already experienced living in a foster family. This reveals that all children, simultaneously and successively, have to deal with plural parents.

Apart from fosterage related to schooling, children often reside with foster parents for reasons associated with marriage and kinship. Firstly, children can be fostered to escape co-wife rivalry and dangerous witchcraft practices in their parents' polygynous households. Secondly, the considerable flexibility of the polygynous system results in high rates of foster children, since mothers divorce easily or abandon their husbands temporarily, thereby habitually leaving their children with the father and a stepmother. Thirdly, birth parents and foster parents may be lost to poor health or death. The kin network serves as a safety net in which their children can be received. Last but not least, children move between kin houses to express solidarity, to maintain reciprocal kin relations and to strengthen matrilineal family ties. It is for example, common practice for brothers to foster their children with barren sisters.

Movement is the first lesson by which children become acquainted with plural parenthood. When children reach the age of two and they cease to be breastfed, they are no longer allowed to constantly enjoy close contact with the birth mother. They are, for instance, sent to a relative to have a good cry, in order for them to start comprehending that they cannot fully claim their mother anymore and to familiarise themselves with plural parenthood. At this age, children can walk and speak and are therefore no longer considered helpless infants in immediate need of parental care. Contrary to what is common practice in our society, with parents often kissing and cudding their growing children and regularly taking them on their lap, in Cameroonian society this behaviour is sternly condemned, as it would not allow children to grow out of infancy. Rather than being considered part of the shared sphere of adults and children, play and intimacy strictly belong to the children's realm. Parents show their protective love towards their children by adopting an authoritarian and distant attitude that is intended to make their children adapt to sudden and often long-term disconnections in the intimate family domain.

Plural parenthood is not only taught in forceful but also in playful ways. When strolling around with their playmates in the district, children stop at related family houses to take a rest, to deliver a message, to enjoy a meal, to offer a helping hand, and at times, to spread a mat to spend the night. When children start attending school, they stay at different places during all school holidays and often spend their leisure time with relatives in the villages. These relatives teach the children about kinship ideology and kinship terms and introduce them to skills like fishing, hunting, gathering and cultivating the fields. Children generally enjoy their stay in the villages where they are easily taken up in their peer group.

By being in various parental contexts, children learn to accept the authority of other parents and to abide by the reciprocal rule that children receive food, clothing and shelter from parents in exchange for obedience and assistance. Children simultaneously learn to distinguish between proper and less appropriate parents in their extended kin network. Though children in a polygynous society have numerous 'fathers' and 'mothers', only their parents' siblings who have the same mother are considered good and reliable foster parents. It is through tasting good food that children acquire a taste for good parenthood. When a child receives no food or only gets bad or poisoned food, it learns that the mother cannot be trusted. In cases that food is good, the kinship bond also tastes good and the mother is considered a reliable one.

Learning plural parenthood through food practices also enables children to constantly revise their opinion of which adults make good parents. In a society where marriages are constantly broken up or expanded, children have to adapt to changing household compositions and re-adjust their view on good parenthood. As long as a maternal aunt stays unmarried, she is an ideal mother to grow up with, as she will see the child as her own and spoil it with good food. However, when she gets married, her husband may be unhappy with the child and hence might refuse to give financial support to feed it. As soon as food gets bad and the child's protection becomes weak, the child is allowed the leave the foster parents and to move to another kin house.

The transmission of kinship knowledge is a continuing process of experiential learning, as Borsboom also vividly describes for the Aboriginal children in Australia (2006). At an ideological level, both mothers and children agree that fosterage is an accepted form of child rearing meant to strengthen family ties and to solve family crises. At the level of everyday practice and the emotions involved, both women and children may however experience difficulties in coping with this practice throughout their life. One woman, pregnant for the third time, told me that she accepted the rules of fosterage when she allowed her husband to foster her first two children with his barren sisters. 'Every woman knows,' she said, 'that you never give birth to a child for yourself, that your child belongs to the whole family.' Pointing at her belly she added: 'But I hope that this one will stay with me, that this pregnancy finally will be in my favour.'

Just as mothers' feelings may differ from normative discourse on rearing practices, children's emotions may also be ambivalent. Let us, to conclude, listen to the story of Serge, a fourteen-year-old boy who adapted to plural parenthood in his early childhood but still longingly recalls his first mother:

I have grown up with two mothers, because my father married his second wife when I was still a small boy. His second wife always ill-treated me. Before being giving any food, I had to work hard. When she behaved like that, my mother got angry at her. The two mothers were always fighting. When my father told his second wife to treat us well, she refused to give us food when we returned from school. Our mother told us not to work for her and to refuse her meals, as she was afraid that she would kill us with poisoned food. My mother gave us food every day, even when it was her co-wife's duty to cook for the whole family. My mother escaped the problems five years ago. She entered into another marriage and fostered us with our maternal grandmother with whom I feel at ease. Nobody wishes to harm us; nobody is fighting; nobody threatens us with witchcraft. It is a calm and safe place. But I still don't understand why our mother left us. She never explained this to us. Five years passed by without seeing her. She lives very far from our place and her husband doesn't welcome us. My mother gave birth to another seven children with her new husband. When I think of her, I feel pain. I need to see her, but she never passes by to visit us. And I have no money to pay the bus fare to go and see her.

Intensively learning kinship rules and practices by means of changing places and tasting food does not routinely adapt people's feelings to the practice. The pain of being disconnected may be felt during a considerable number of years. However, kinship knowledge also enables the children to find their own way in the extended kin network by giving them, at the age of ten, the opportunity to choose their foster parents themselves. Playful wandering through the district then tranforms into a serious nomadic life style that leads the growing children to the big cities throughout the whole country and even to the European metropoles.

REFERENCES

Borsboom, A. 2006 [1996]. *De clan van de Wilde Honing: Spirituele rijkdom van de Aborigines* Haarlem, Binkey Kok.

Fieldwork in Manus, Papua New Guinea: On Change, Exchange and Anthropological Knowledge

Ton Otto

When I was about to leave the island of Baluan in 1988, after two years of fieldwork, the old woman Alup Nakeau gave me a special gift. It was large polished shell knife, called *yanul*, that according to traditional rules could be used only by *lapans* – that are traditional leaders – to cut and distribute a bunch of betelnut on ceremonial occasions (Ohnemus 1996). Alup Nakeau was then the oldest living member of the Sauka clan into which I had been adopted. She was the eldest child of Ninou Solok, who had been the last acknowledged lapan of the Sauka. The *yanul* not only connects me to Ninou Solok but through him also to an important event in the cultural history of the island.

In order to explain the importance of this event I have to sketch a little bit of the preceding cultural history of the island. Baluan is the birth place of Paliau Maloat, a political and religious reformer who has become very well-known in comparative studies of religious movements thanks to the work of Margaret Mead (especially 1956) and Theodore Schwartz (1962), see also Otto (1992a, 1998). After the Second World War, which had a great impact on Manus, Paliau succeeded in mobilising a large number of villages in a truly revolutionary reform movement. The overall aim of the movement was to become equal with the white colonisers. Paliau claimed to have received direct access to the same kind of knowledge that had made the white people so rich and powerful. He started to reorganise village life according to models he had learned while serving as a sergeant in the colonial constabulary. An important focus of his reform was the abolition of local traditions, which he thought were hampering progress. In particular the spectacular *lapan* feasts with the butchery of large numbers of pigs and the elaborate marriage ceremonies had to be discontinued because they were considered a waste of wealth and energy. This revolutionary restructuring had an enormous impact on social relations as local traditional leaders were deprived of one of their most important means of asserting their status. Kinship ties and obligations were de-emphasised in favour of the communal organisation of work under a new kind of political leadership. It appears that the New Way, as the cultural reform was called, mobilised sufficient popular support to enforce and sustain the new type of social relations for at least a decade. Marriages were confirmed in a short ceremony in the presence of a local 'councillor' through the presentation of a token bride price of 10 Australian pounds. The great *lapan* feasts, which had been a focal point of the pre-war culture, were abolished completely.

In the late 1950s a counter movement gained in force. Ninou Solok of the big Sauka clan was the first to openly organise a large traditional feast in defiance of the elected political leaders. I was told that he did this after having been hit by a falling branch from a nut tree. Acutely aware of the fragility of life he wanted to establish his own reputation ('name') and reassert that of his clan by organising a big ceremony. He persuaded his clan members and affines to plant a number of very large gardens with yams, the kind of food that was especially valued according to tradition. When these tubers were ripe he distributed the food to the children of Sauka women who had married into other clans, the so-called *narumpein*. The distribution ceremony was accompanied with elaborate dancing and singing and received the name of a song, namely *polpolot*. The *narumpein* returned the gift of yams with some dog's teeth and shell money, the traditional valuables, but mainly with Western money. Ninou Solok distributed the money equally among his affines, who had supported him, and his clan-brothers, the *narumwen*. At these occasions of giving and receiving the *lapan* would open the ceremony with a distribution of betelnut, a sign of his leadership. And it is for dividing the betelnut that Ninou Solok most likely used the *yanul* now in my possession.

Ninou Solok's example was followed by the traditional leaders of several other big clans who organised *polpolots* in the following years. The culture historical importance of this event was that it marked the beginning of a long-lasting and still on-going revival and revaluation of tradition on Baluan (Otto 1991, 1992b, 2002). In several ways the *polpolot* was not traditional in a strict sense. It was not connected to one of the main transitions in life – birth, marriage or death – as most traditional ceremonies had been, nor did it closely resemble a *lapan* feast. Nevertheless the *polpolot* was experienced as traditional, because it re-established the importance of gift giving between kin and revived the use of kinship categories such as *narumwen* and *narumpein*. I have never met Ninou Solok, since he died before I arrived on Baluan but I have talked with other leaders of those early *polpolot* ceremonies. They motivated their actions by referring to a need to 'show their family', as they called it. In addition it was considered as a successful attempt to assert their clan leadership through organizing the exchange of gifts.

Several factors at a regional and even international scale contributed to the increasing relevance that was attached to 'tradition', but my little example should suffice to show that purely local factors played an important role as well. I refer in particular to an inertia of cultural models ingrained in people's habitus, which makes it difficult if not impossible for any revolution to change social relations instantly and completely. Changing the visible external relations does not immediately lead to changes in cultural perceptions, values and notions of agency. In addition my example underlines the importance of the micro-politics of local actors who strive for culturally valued status and who use the cultural resources that are at hand. The case of Ninou Solok's *polpolot* serves as an illustration of my ongoing attempts to analyse and theorise cultural change (cf. Borsboom 1986; Otto and Borsboom 1997). Clearly this revival of tradition is an instance of cultural change, which at the same time highlights the persistence of cultural models.

But let me return to Alup Nakeau from whom I received the *yanul* in order to further trace the exchange networks in which a fieldwork anthropologist becomes entangled. Alup Nakeau visited me in my house after I had given a large farewell party in which about 250 people had participated. She presented me with a traditional earthen pot and with the *yanul* of her father Ninou Solok. The farewell party had been a culmination of my gradual integration into local social networks. When I arrived on the island two years previously, I became soon involved in local ceremonial exchanges. I had introduced myself as someone who was interested in documenting local customs and history. Therefore I was frequently called to attend gift exchanges of various kinds. After a while my wife and I became drawn into these gift exchanges, because we started to receive a small share of the food distributed. Such ceremonial exchanges are key social events and all the gifts are displayed and divided into heaps which acknowledge the positions of the various receivers. The anthropologist and his wife became such a receiver and concomitantly also a unit with obligations to give in return. This marked the first stage of our integration into local exchange networks.

Later on we became even more closely integrated, when I was publicly given a name and position within the Sauka clan. The new situation allowed me to pursue a more thorough exploration of the complexities of gift giving than I had previously achieved. Until then I had observed many exchanges and interviewed many of the knowledgeable people involved. Nevertheless I had not discovered that a part of the ceremony occurred at night, hidden from the eyes of the public. Under the cover of darkness the central recipients would receive an additional gift, because during daytime they were expected to demonstrate their generosity by distributing most or even all of what they had received. This fact had never been mentioned to me, nor had I ever thought of asking about such a possibility. Once I was part of the kin network, I was naturally introduced to this part of the ceremony and also to many other aspects of sharing and mutual obligation.

The celebrated expression 'participant observation' is often used to refer to what an anthropologist does in the field. In fact the term covers a variety of ways to collect information and to produce ethnographic knowledge (cf. Otto 1997). Pure observation is based on the categories, which the researcher has formulated in advance. It implies a certain distance to the observed social reality. Via interviews, probably the most important tool for most ethnographers, the researcher is able to explore local categories and interpretations. This technique has a bias towards knowledge that can be expressed in words. As illustrated in my example, the researcher is limited by what he can ask and by what his informants find relevant to convey. Finally there is the method of participation or 'role play', in which the researcher gets more deeply involved in local social relations. This gives the possibility of a more subjective experience of local cultural notions and traditions. All three research strategies mentioned involve negotiations with the local people about access, exchange and interpretation. All three constitute forms of knowledge in their own right, which have to be integrated to produce a comprehensive ethnographic picture.

I believe that organising the farewell party provided me with a chance to experience some of the cultural values that motivate Baluan men to engage in large ceremonial exchanges. It also provided me with a keen insight into the many difficulties and risks involved. But if one succeeds, one is richly awarded. In my case I was able 'to show' my Sauka family, who strongly supported the enterprise. It demonstrated the power of kin relations and the involved reciprocal obligations. In addition I enjoyed the 'name' or reputation that comes with such an achievement, which is an important social value on Baluan. The success of the farewell party was apparently the reason for Alup Nakeau to give me her father's *yanul*. She said that none of her brothers had been able to organise a major feast. My farewell party however had reminded her of her father's *polpolot* and had reinstalled her pride in being a member of the Sauka clan.

Later I gave her the Swiss knife I had used in the field. When I returned four years later, one of her sons approached me. He said: 'Our mother has passed away'. He showed the Swiss knife which she had cherished until her death and which he had inherited. The two types of knives connect different people and different contexts. For me the *yanul* represents my links with the Sauka clan on Baluan and the importance of gift exchanges which tie people together in networks that define their position and personhood (cf. Strathern 1988). It also evokes social change and the feast organised by Ninou Solok half a century ago. The Swiss knife embodies the presence of my wife and me on the island of Baluan and the relationships we have maintained. As such it is a gift just as the *yanul*, but is also maintains some of the imageries of a commodity, produced and bought in the West, a sign of a faraway world with nearly unlimited possibilities.

REFERENCES

Borsboom, A. 1986. 'The Cultural Dimensions of Change: An Australian Example' *Anthropos* 81: 605-615.

Mead, M. 1956. *New Lives for Old: Cultural Transformation - Manus, 1928-1953* London, Victor Gollancz.

Ohnemus, S. 1996. *Zur Kultur der Admiralitäts-Insulaner in Melanesien: Die Sammlung Alfred Bühler im Museum für Völkerkunde Basel* Basel, Museum für Völkerkunde.

Otto, T. 1991. *The Politics of Tradition in Baluan: Social Change and the Construction of the Past in Manus* Nijmegen, Centre for Pacific Studies.

Otto, T. 1992a. 'The Paliau Movement in Manus and the Objectification of Tradition' *History and Anthropology* 5: 427-454.

Otto, T. 1992b. 'The Ways of Kastam: Tradition as Category and Practice in a Manus Village' *Oceania* 62: 264-283.

Otto, T. 1997. 'Informed Participation and Participating Informants' *Canberra Anthropology* 20, 1-2: 96-108.

Otto, T. 1998. 'Paliau's Stories: Autobiography and Automythography of a Melanesian Prophet' *Focaal* 32: 71-87.

Otto, T. 2002. 'Chefs, big men et bureaucrates: Weber et les politiques de la tradition à Baluan (Papouasie, Nouvelle-Guinée)' eds. C. Hamelin and E. Wittersheim *La tradition et l'État: Églises, pouvoirs et politiques culturelles dans le Pacifique* Paris, L'Harmattan: 103-129.

Otto, T. and A. Borsboom eds. 1997. *Cultural Dynamics of Religious Change in Oceania* Leiden, KITLV Press.

Schwartz, T. 1962. 'The Paliau Movement in the Admiralty Islands, 1946-54' *Anthropological Papers of the American Museum of Natural History* 49: 207-421.

Strathern, M. 1988. *The Gender of the Gift: Problems with Women and Problems with Society in Melanesia* Berkeley, University of California Press.

Bodily Learning:
The Case of Pilgrimage by Foot
to Santiago de Compostela

Janneke Peelen

Why do so many people in this day and age walk the pilgrimage route to Santiago de Compostela? Does the endeavor entail a learning experience? And if so, what kind of learning? Having made the 'sacred' journey to the pilgrimage centre on foot myself, I want to answer these questions on the basis of my own experiences and those of fellow pilgrims, whom I encountered during the course of my hiking tour.

The age-old pilgrimage road to Santiago de Compostela is commonly known as the *camino* ('road' or 'way' in Spanish). In recent years, walking the *camino* has regained a great deal of its past luster and popularity. Nowadays, the pilgrimage route that ends in the northwest of Spain attracts people – young and old, male and female, religious and non-religious – from around the world. Rather than its destination, Santiago's Cathedral with the relics of the apostle Saint James, it is the long and winding *camino* itself that inspires them to make the pilgrimage.[28] This route, more than any other contemporary pilgrimage track in Europe, is characterized by long-distance walking (Peelen and Jansen f.c.). In images of olden times, the pilgrims on their way to Santiago use to be depicted in a romantic fashion with a wide mantle, a large hat decorated with a cockleshell, a calabash for drinking water, and a long staff (referring to Saint James). Surprisingly, the modern-day pilgrims' attire has not changed as much as one would expect. The latter closely resemble their forebearers in outlook with their backpacks decorated with a cockleshell,

---

[28] Over 80 percent of the annual pilgrims to Santiago walk, whereas the remainder go the distance by bike, on horseback or in a wheelchair. These statistics, however, exclude the pilgrims who visit Santiago by other means of transport, for instance, by car, bus or airplane.

the hats protecting them against the sun, sports coats, water bottles, and walking sticks.

What motivates so many to embark on the approximately 750 kilo-metres hike to Santiago is first and foremost the *camino*'s healing power.[29] These pilgrims seek an all-embracing or holistic sort of healing. Their ailments are not of a physical nature, but concern other types of suffering, so to speak, in the emotional, social and/or spiritual realm. In order to grasp the nature of the healing process involved, it is necessary to consider the impact that walking the long distance has on the pilgrims. Furthermore, the *camino* can be identi-fied as a ritualized space on which numerous previous pilgrims as well as co-pilgrims during the same time span have left their mark. On the personal level, due to the strenuous walk, pilgrims frequently get in touch again with their physical body and with their own selves (Peelen and Jansen f.c.). The body, as perceived or experienced, becomes a vehicle for personal growth and an important source of self-awareness (Blacking 1977; Frey 1998; Sklar 2001). In understanding the process of bodily learning, Ad Borsboom's work (1978, 1994, 2006) on the importance of the body and bodily movement in Aboriginal ritual is very inspiring. His analysis of the body as bearer of (cultural) knowledge is very useful for understanding the bodily aspects of ritual in general.

The ritualized walking of the *camino* brings forth a learning process by means of both bodily movement and the sense of an inter-connectedness with other pilgrims, past and present, to which the road bears testimony. In many respects, the pilgrimage route is a discursive space, a chain of pilgrims' stories that highlight the route's religious and spiritual significance as well as its healing powers. The traces of earlier pilgrims provide a physical underpinning to these stories. They are present not only in small roadside monuments and in road markers, but can also be found in monasteries, churches and bridges that have been built for the sake of the pilgrimage. When they walk the *camino*, pilgrims anticipate these stories. Moreover, the so-

---

[29] The point of departure as well as the precise distance travelled on foot is a matter of the pilgrims' own preferences. However, if time allows, most start walking near the Pyrenees in France, at the beginning of the so-called *camino frances*, at a distance of around 750 kilo-metres from Santiago de Compostela.

called Santiago institution induces them to take the special nature of the walking trip into account. This entails, amongst others, that all pilgrims carry a pilgrim passport, identifying them as a 'pilgrim', and that they follow designated routes, while making use of the institutional provisions for pilgrims, such as hostels set up along the way (Peelen and Jansen f.c.). On the road they thus learn what it means to be a pilgrim, while concurrently they cannot but connect themselves with past, present, and future pilgrims. The pilgrims' personal experiences do become part and parcel of the phenomenon of the *camino*.

Pilgrims appear to grasp the route's significance mediated through their body. The manner in which people walk – their rhythm and bodily posture – reveals a great deal about their inner life. Space does not allow me to give more than just one example to illuminate this point. Peter and Jessy, a couple from Canada, related to me how they learned 'the hard way' – by suffering bodily injuries – that life requires making choices. They could not simply decide to walk longer distances and at a faster pace without eventually having to pay a price. They commenced their journey in Le Puy in France, having had eight weeks' time at their disposal to accomplish it. Initially they went slowly as they did not aim to reach Santiago de Compostela at all costs. After a couple of weeks, however, they changed their minds and increased their walking pace to ascertain they would arrive at the pilgrimage centre before the end of their holiday. Halfway through, however, they both were in bad shape: '[After a day of walking] we had long soaks and lay on the bed, barely managing to rise to our feet to make supper – using the supplies we had brought with us, such as tasty bread, blue cheese, apples, and milk – at about 8.30 pm. Next, we went off to bed at 9.30 pm. If we hadn't had the food, we probably would not have eaten a thing. We didn't have the emotional energy to get out of the room. At that point, it dawned upon us that we had to reduce our pace and that we would not make it to Santiago.' Later on, Jessy and Peter acceded that they would apply the lessons learned from their exhausted bodies to the way they intended to live the remainder of their lives. They had become well aware that you have to bear the consequences of every step in life you take, and this not only in a literal sense.

Overcoming the physical challenges of the *camino* often results in enhanced self-confidence. Isabel, a pilgrim from Australia, went away with a useful guideline for everyday life. She compared the mountains of the *camino* with the 'hills' she had to mount at home. Isabel told me that every time (in walking the *camino*) she had to climb a mountain, she looked towards the ground in front of her, observing her steps. Isabel felt that when she would look further afield, she would never get anywhere. Step by step, however, she slowly moved forwards, and time and again her body transported her to another mountain top. Isabel was twenty-one years of age when I became acquainted with her and her daily struggles. She said she had recently recovered from an alcohol and drug addiction. Although Isabel had been clean for over year, she had a hard time trying to find a (new) purpose in life. In her assessment of her *camino*-experiences, she claimed it had taught her that at home she too would have to take life on a day-to-day basis. Step by step, and not looking to far ahead, every other day would take her one further step away from her old habits. Her confidence in her own strength had waxed as a result of her physically and mentally conquering the mountains of the *camino*.

These and other stories that various pilgrims shared with me demonstrate that for them the movement of the body served as an important learning device (see also Rosaldo 1986), often providing them a deeper understanding of the self, their social relationships, and new outlooks on the world around them. It is hardly surprising that pilgrims frequently express that upon returning home they feel a healing has taken place. The present revival of the pilgrimage by foot, I found (see also Peelen 2006), is closely related to a quest for a bodily learning process as described. The 'modern' pilgrimage to Santiago de Compostela probably has gained its renewed significance, because such experiences are not to be had in the humdrum of everyday life nor in walks with less spiritual overtones.

The body as a 'conduit of knowledge' has also a bearing on the methods that can be employed by anthropologists. All too often the researcher's own bodily experiences and sentiments are excluded from the research and the resulting data. I would like to propose a more intimate research method, in line with the need to show empathy, by making use of the experience of one's own body for the sake of an improved understanding of our subjects, the people we study, especially in the field of ritual studies.[30] On the one hand, every single person will have his or her own bodily experiences, and will reflect on these personal experiences guided by one's specific background and upbringing. On the other hand, the bodily experiences in ritual (including the ritualized walking of the *camino*) are commonly shared, because they emerge and are interpreted in a particular sociocultural context (see also Dubisch 1995). Therefore such experiences, as related by people and had by the analyst, have a tremendous potential of increasing our understanding of what makes pilgrims 'tick'. One thing is certain: if I had not submitted myself to a similar physical regime as other pilgrims, I would have gained a far less thorough insight into their learning processes. Every single step I took along the lengthy *camino*, as a pilgrim among pilgrims, helped me to get closer to what pilgrimage is about for many of my fellow travellers.

References

Blacking, J. ed. 1977. *The Anthropology of the Body*. London, Academic Press.

Borsboom, A. 1978. *Maradjiri: A Modern Ritual Complex in Arnhem Land, North Australia*. Nijmegen, Katholieke Universiteit Nijmegen, PhD thesis.

Borsboom, A. 1994. 'Gedragingen rond het sterven. Dodenriten bij Australische Aborigines' eds H. Driessen and H. de Jonge. *In de ban van betekenis: Proeven van symbolische antropologie* Nijmegen, SUN.

Borsboom. A. 2006. *De clan van de Wilde Honing: Spirituele rijkdom van de Aborigines* Haarlem, Binkey Kok.

Brown, K.M. 2001. *Mama Lola: A Vodou Priestess in Brooklyn* Berkely, University of California Press.

Dubisch, J. 1995. *In a Different Place: Pilgrimage, Gender, and Politics at a Greek Island Shrine* Princeton, Princeton University Press.

Dubisch, J. 2004. '"Heartland of America": Memory, Motion and the (Re)construction of History on a Motorcycle Pilgrimage' eds. S. Coleman and J. Eade *Reframing Pilgrimage: Cultures in Motion* London, Routledge: 105-132.

Frey, N.L. 1998. *Pilgrim Stories: On and off the Road to Santiago* Berkely, University of California Press.

Peelen, J. 2006. *Lopend stilstaan bij je leven: Pelgrims onderweg naar Santiago de Compostela* Nijmegen, Radboud Universiteit, MA thesis

---

[30] This personal and intimate involvement increasingly finds its way through in anthropological works. Some inspiring works are those of Brown (2001), Dubisch (1995, 2004), Rosaldo (1984), Sklar (2001), Stoller and Olkes (1987).

Peelen, J. and W. Jansen. f.c. 'Emotive Movement on the Road to Santiago de Compostela' *Etnofoor*.

Rosaldo, R. 1984. 'Grief and a Headhunter's Rage: On the Cultural Force of Emotions' eds. S. Plattner and E. Bruner *Text, Play, and Story: The Construction of Self and Society* Washington, American Ethnological Society: 178-195.

Rosaldo, R. 1986. 'Ilongot Hunting as Story and Experience' eds. V. W. Turner and E. M. Bruner *The Anthropology of Experience* Urbana, University of Illinois Press: 97-138.

Sklar, D. 2001. *Dancing with the Virgin: Body and Faith in the Fiesta of Tortugas, New Mexico* Berkely, California Press.

Stoller, P. and C. Olkes. 1987. *In Sorcery's Shadow: A Memoir of Apprenticeship among the Shonghay in Niger* Chicago, University of Chicago Press.

Just Humming:
The Consequence of the Decline of Learning Contexts among the Warlpiri

Nicolas Peterson

In February 2006, the antipodean summer, I arrived at the Aboriginal village of Yuendumu, 300km northwest of Alice Springs to continue work on a project to record, transcribe and translate song cycles sung by Warlpiri speakers. This was, in part, to follow up on many hours of recordings made during fieldwork in 1972-3, which had been neglected since then. The summer period from December to February is the time that Warlpiri people have conducted circumcision cere-monies as part of male maturity rites, at least since their involvement with the pastoral industry, because it was the period of the summer lay off from stock work. I arrived just after the last ceremonies of that year had finished, as I learnt from an old Aboriginal friend. I asked him about the ceremonies, where they had been held, who had been involved and whether they had been conducted in the same way as when I first saw them in 1972. After a few minutes of answering my questions he halted and then said: you know those younger and middle-aged people don't know the songs, they were 'just humming'.

This surprised me. Warlpiri people are not in decline, indeed their numbers are growing substantially, with over 800 Warlpiri speakers living at Yuendumu and several hundred other Warlpiri people nearby. Further it was not as if there had been a hiatus in the holding of circumcision between 1973 and 2006. Not only have circumcision ceremonies been held at Yuendumu during most Christmas periods but they have also been held at nearby Wurriwurri (Mt Allen Station), the home of Amatjirra speakers, which Warlpiri often participated in. Further in many years substantial numbers of Warlpiri people have been gathered up by travelling pre-circumcision candidates (jilkaja) and their guardians from other communities, sometimes from communities over a thousand kilometres away, and taken back to the boys home community to participate in the ceremony for the boy held there. While there is some variation in the main circumcision ceremony held across the Western Desert there is enough similarity in language, song and ceremony for people from far apart to fully participate in each others ceremonies.

Up until the late 1970s Warlpiri male maturity rites, which have been well described by Mervyn Meggitt in his classic work, Desert People (1962), generally involved two and not more than three boys being circumcised at the same time, making them yalpuru (co-initates) and life time friends. During the thirteen months I lived at Yuendumu with my wife in 1972-3, there were three separate circumcision ceremonies, and Yuendumu was visited by two jilkaja parties, one taking a relatively small group of some thirty or forty people off to La Grange on the coast of Western Australia and a much more localised one to the neighbouring Aboriginal village of Papunya some 90 km to the south, which well over a hundred people from Yuendumu attended.

People enjoyed and still enjoy the circumcision ceremony even though each ceremony is quite arduous. Thee is ceremonial activity during the day with men and women in separate groups, but in sight of each other, followed by a night during which the men sing from around 10pm till dawn while the women dance. On the second night, a few days later, people do get to sleep after a lot of complex ritual activity and singing and dancing with the final proceedings taking place at dusk the following day. This ceremony in its fullest form is the peak of Warlpiri high culture.

So the question is what has happened over the last thirty years in the transmission of the songs that could have resulted in many people just humming rather than singing.

One set of issues relates to greatly increased mobility over the last 30 years, now that people have easy access to cars, and as a consequence much easier access to town and alcohol. This means that it is harder to keep the substantial numbers of people that are needed to hold the ceremonies around, or to depend on them being available. Nevertheless many of the younger men have been present at the ceremonies, danced in them and played other roles on a number of occasions, especially where the ceremony involved their close kin.

This suggests that there are other issues relating to the learning and performance context. Although there are several different ceremonies at which boys may be circumcised there are only two minor variations of the song line associated with the main form of the ceremony used at Yuendumu, so it seems unlikely that for any person keen to learn the songs there has not been the opportunity to do so. In 2007 I witnessed a ceremony which was the last one in the season and only held because the boy's mother had not been available earlier as a result of sickness. Because boys are very rarely circumcised singly, indeed, only as a punishment in a truncated form of the ceremony in my experience, two other boys were found to be circumcised at the same time. The attendance was quite small with only 16 adult men and around 30 adult women, making the ceremony much more the sort of size it would have been long ago. Only six of the men carried the singing. They sat together in a tight circle and on the western side facing east sat the ten other men close to them. The men in the central circle were all over 50 while those sitting outside the circle would have ranged in age from early twenties to late forties, with one man possibly older. The men in the outer circle sometimes hummed, sometimes they sang along for one or two versus but much of the time they sat silently or talked quietly among themselves. The six men in the central circle represented at least half of the men in that age bracket at Yuendumu and were there because of their kin relationship to the boys. Of the older men who might have been there two were absent because they were ill and infirm. This gathering underlined a significant change that has taken place over the last 30 years.

My field notes from 1972-1973 show there were substantially more older men around then than the dozen or so who are alive today. This reflects the big change in the age structure of the Aboriginal population that has taken place over the last thirty years. Speaking impressionistically, it is clear that the numbers of people 55 and over has declined as a proportion of the population. This has been brought about because people have become a lot less healthy between then and now and the morbidity rate has increased dramatically so that few people make it beyond their 50s. This is widely lamented and commented on by both the Aboriginal people and health authorities. The older generation had led a harder life, often on the cattle stations in the region and was always fitter and more active than people today. Even though their diet, up to the 1970s, was largely made up of flour, tea, sugar, jam and meat, it was a lot healthier than that which people have now with easy access to junk and fast foods and huge quantities of soft drinks that all add up to a really poor diet and a great deal of obesity.

So what has happened is that there are not only not enough older people to socialise the younger generations in the more esoteric aspect of Warlpiri culture but the proportion of the population in the younger generations has greatly increased with strong population growth throughout the last thirty years. A consequence for the circumcision ceremonies is that on most occasions many more than three boys are circumcised at the same ceremony, indeed as many as seventeen boys have been recorded at a single ceremony at Yuen-dumu. This is because the few older people needed to maintain the singing all night are not up to doing it on several consecutive occasions. If they were to stick to separate ceremonies for every two to three boys the changed demographics would mean as many as eight ceremonies each Christmas period that would rely on the same six to ten men at Yuendumu. These senior men can call on a few older people from neighbouring communities on some occasions, but it is clear that the strain is too large. May be part of the loss of knowledge is due to younger men only attending the occasional ceremony that involved their very close relatives in which they are obliged to perform certain roles, and unlike the older generation they have not automatically attended one or more ceremonies every year. There is also the issue of respect for age and the feeling of the younger men that they are too young for it to be appropriate for them to play an active part in the singing yet. As a consequence of these and possibly other factors too, not only the songs but the current forms of the ceremony are under real threat.

REFERENCES

Meggitt, M.J. 1962. *Desert People: A Study of the Walbiri Aborigines of Central Australia* Sydney, Angus and Robertson.

A Note on Observation

Anton Ploeg

In his major book, *The Wild Honey Clan*, Ad Borsboom discusses several strategies that Australian Aborigines employ to transmit knowledge, without making use of written messages. He mentions the use of a variety of metaphors, and the imagining of such metaphors in stories and dances, that are, moreover, regularly told and performed (2006: 101f). In this brief note I shift the focus to the role of observation, in part because during my research among the Western Dani, I did not acquire the linguistic facility to record long stories, in part because I focus on other types of knowledge, and, maybe, in part because of different cultural orientations among the peoples concerned.

In 1960, while preparing for my field work among the Western Dani, I presumed that I would learn a great deal about their way of life by observing how young Dani were taught skills by their elders. This presumption did not come true at all. Shortly after my arrival among the Wanggulam, the group of Dani among whom I had decided to work, they started preparing a new set of food gardens. Much of the work was done by parties of men helping each other on a reciprocal basis. Although they worked together in the same locality and on the same job, for instance cutting trees and removing undergrowth, they did so independently, by themselves.

That appeared most strikingly during fence building. Dani fences, serving to keep pigs out of food gardens, are sturdy structures. They consist of roughly adzed, irregularly shaped planks, put horizontally on top of each other, and held in place by vertical poles on either side of the planks. They were tied together with rattan. On top short poles are put crosswise and the structure is topped off by a mixture of grasses, vines and other small plants to protect it against the heavy rains. Each man built a separate section of the fence, about three meters long. Having finished that section, he might start building another, a bit further on. Never did I see a young man helping another man so as to learn on the job. They all seemed to be knowledgeable fence builders.

One of the few times that I was formally instructed myself, took place during a pandanus meal. For Wanggulam oil pandanus was a delicacy. They mixed the oil with solid food such as mashed sweet potatoes or bananas in oblong, shallow wooden bowls, a noticeable part of their material culture. The bowls were carefully adzed and polished, while the interior often had a reddish shine produced by the many oil pandanus dishes they had contained. The oil of oil pandanus is contained in a multitude of tiny seeds, almost always deep red, set on oblong drupes. After steaming in an earth oven, the oil can be pressed out of the seeds. This is done by taking handfuls of seeds, and applying pressure clasping one's hands together. After I had done this on a few occasions, it was gently made clear to me that I did it wrongly. The idea was to shake the oil of one's hands without spattering and that required some training. I never saw other men getting advice about it. But on one occasion returning home from a visit with a companion, I noticed a youngster at some distance from the path where we walked. Since he had his back towards us, he did not see us. He squatted near a mud pool and pressed mud from between his hands as if he were pressing oil from pandanus seeds. My companion confirmed that this was the way youngsters acquired the skill. Hence socialisation among the Wanggulam required that those who wanted to become socialised, who wanted to acquire the skills that participation in adult life presupposed, took initiative.

I am not sure to what extent a lack of formal instruction in technical skills is or was a feature of other New Guinean ways of life. However there are other examples. The first I mention has been reported by Maureen MacKenzie who researched the significance of looped string bags, *bilum* in Tok Pisin, *noken* in Indonesian, in the life of the Telefol, in the Highlands of Papua New Guinea, not far from the border with West Papua.[31] Bilum were then, and probably still are, the indispensable carrying implement of the Telefol, of Telefol women especially. Mackenzie first states that girls acquired the skill by observation (1991: 100). They got ample opportunity, since looping string bags and twining the string required was part of everyday life. But there was more to it than mere observation. A

---

[31] Miekee Kijne reminded me of these comments by MacKenzie.

Telefol woman told Mackenzie that she had wanted to continue work on the string bag that her mother was working on and that she had left behind in the house. But she made a mess of it and it took her mother hours to undo what she had done wrong. In her own words her mother told her

> You must start a training *bilum* of your own, you want to make a *bilum*, but your hands are heavy. You must practise to get the proper feel of looping. When you have made your first *bilum* it will be cranky, but then we will throw it in the river. The river will carry your wonky *bilum* away and it will wash away your heavy handed-ness (MacKenzie 1991: 102).

A second example I mention concerns the evaluation of cowrie shells among the Me, formerly called Kapauku or Ekagi, living in the western tip of the Highlands of West Papua. At the time Europeans contacted the Me, in the late 1930's, the Me were fascinated by the cowrie shells that they used as payments or prestations in transactions. Shells were ranked according to their physical properties and further differentiated within ranks. High ranking shells were worth a multiple of low ranking ones. After Europeans had introduced cowries and, later, western currency, cowries remained in use in transactions, in part as a result of a new differentiation between 'old' and 'new' shells, the latter category being shells that were imported by people working for the colonial institutions. Accordingly, when Sibbele Hylkema, a Franciscan missionary, started ethnographic work among the Me in 1969, he was able to observe how the Me then used their cowries.

A problem that puzzled him for a long time was by what criteria Me ranked their cowries. Accordingly he urged his Me research assistant to ask his father, one of the experts, how he assessed the rank and the value of a cowrie. The older man just said: *'dou'*, 'you look'. This remark, Hylkema observes, was in line with the Me tenet that people learn by observation. As regards fence building, one of the examples I mentioned for the Wanggulam, Hylkema writes that one learns by looking on, or, more likely, by inspecting later on, out of the sight of others, how the fence had been built. When Hylkema and his assistant met the latter's father on a later occasion, he explic-itly mentioned a few of the criteria that he applied. His wife told her son to carefully inspect those cowries that experts had judged as excellent. She took part in cowrie transactions, but for ranking had to rely on the advice of others.

Hylkema noticed an incongruity between the considerable length of time that Me, also the experts, needed to come up with an assess-ment and the briefness of their spoken verdict. So he opines that Me were unable to verbalise the reasons why they assigned a specific rank to a cowrie. Hence, even if they had wanted, experts would have been unable to pass their expertise on to pupils in oral communication. However, Hylkema makes it clear that young Me men were disin-clined to become pupils. As he writes:

> However, even at a very young age, it no longer fits a man to be lectured. The word *tedemai*, to be lectured, has a pejorative ring, synonymous with docility and obedience. Stereotypically this behaviour is demanded from women. One does not question because one does not want to be lectured. On the other hand, people do not appreciate to be questioned. To be questioned comes close to being under scrutiny... or to being threatened in a monopoly in a closely guarded expertise (Hylkema n.d.: Ch. 9, my translation).

Hylkema had the benefit of very long-term field work and apparently was fluent in the Me language, conditions that do not apply to my own research among the Wanggulam. But it seems plausible to me that analogous considerations shackled formal instruction among them.

REFERENCES

Borsboom, A. 2006 [1996]. *De clan van de Wilde Honing: Spirituele rijkdom van de Aborigines* Haarlem, Binkey Kok, 3rd edition.

Hylkema, S. n.d. *Cowries and Brideprice among the Me or Ekagi, Central Highlands, West Papua* edited, annotated and concluded by A. Ploeg Berlin, Lit Verlag.

MacKenzie, M.A. 1991. *Androgynous Objects: String Bags and Gender in Central New Guinea* Reading, Harwood Academic Publishers.

Fragments of Transmission of Kamoro Culture (South-West Coast, West Papua), Culled from Fieldnotes, 1952-1954

Jan Pouwer

On 13th January 1954 my wife, baby-daughter and I settle down for several months of intensive research on the spot, in a guesthouse in the village of Ipiri, west of the administrative centre of Kaokonao, after a few hours travelling by canoe loaded to the brim with our *barang*. Fortunately the treacherous shallow sea behaves properly this time. On our arrival we learn that Paremakani, a middle-aged man, a reputed singer and drummer, huntsman and fisher is gravely ill, for the second time. He is said to have turned down sound advice by self-righteous wailing relatives and his mother-in law to be transported by his bride taking in-laws – the society's jacks of all trades – to Kaokonao hospital. His illness and his anticipated death is a public event. The hut is crammed with lamenting relatives and friends. His bride taking in-laws are forbidden to partake in wailing lest they want to risk being slapped on the face (which I once noticed). In front of the house wailers come and go, their lamenting time depending on the degree of kinship. Earlier, the sick man has been asked if the ghosts of his late bride taking in-laws have already arrived to take him upstream to the abode of the dead. He then nodded, his staring eyes believed to be flabbergasted by his ghostly companions. Asked again this time there is no answer: he is unconscious. Close relatives and affines move and pinch his head arms and legs in order to implore his wandering soul to return to the body; to no avail. On January 20 in the afternoon some thunderclaps – usual in this period of the season – announce his death. He passes away on 5.30 p.m. His wife, close relatives and affines sitting around the body move his limbs and head in grief. 'The limbs, the head do not stir anymore, life has gone.' Outbursts of wailing last for hours. The widow wallows in the mud and outrageously hacks away at trees and shrubs with a machete. Returning to the body of her husband she throws herself at full length on it, sobbing, wailing and moving his limbs in utter sorrow. So do her children and his sister's children. Amongst them, his son, a schoolboy, who is lifted over the milling crowd and lies on his father, motionless, in grief.

At about 8.30 p.m. the guild of fully dressed singers, of which the deceased was a most distinguished member, turns up at the scene. Wailing stops: this is an important moment. Totòpia, the main singer, performs the first strophe of a significant standard repertoire, part and parcel of the ritual initiation of boys into adolescents, and of adolescents into manhood. Paremakani was especially well versed in this age-old repertoire. The main singer's headdress, consisting of five yellow feathers of a bird-of-paradise, glimmers in the flickering fire in vigorous, rhythmic movements of the head. He is accompanied by the low humming voices of the other singers. With a short nod he invites the next singer to repeat the strophe and so on. The sharp diction, surprising modulations of rhythms and the beautiful falsetto voices of the participants, render this performance of about ten minutes into a perfect piece of beauty (which is a joy for ever). This performance is not just an homage to the deceased – his name is not even mentioned – but is meant as a faultless exercise: making mistakes in text and performance would irritate the ghost (*ipu*) of the deceased; he could make them forget the proper text or even have them sing the wrong words. Now, singers/drummers are accountable. Their social status matches their responsibilities. At ceremonies they are well looked after in terms of food and drinks. They are even entitled to taste the festive food first. Proper transmission by them of proper ritual knowledge, entailed in 'sacred' songs, is vital, lest harm and sickness would be imparted.

Kaokonao, 19 December 1952: I attend the initiation of boys and adolescents. Drumming/singing of ceremonial or casual-everyday texts, often invented on the spot, form a major part of the ritual. I witness how an aged singer formally transmits his function to his teenage son, already thoroughly trained by him. The old singer blows toward his successor's mouth, while mimicking the transfer of songs from his mouth with his right hand. The transmission is irreversible on pain of illness. His son behaves shyly. The latter's bride-taking in-laws assist and support him; in their turn they gesticulate the presentation of songs by *his* mouth. Such a demarcating behaviour is called *kakar* = sign. *Kakari* are manifold in rituals and in everyday life. They highlight orderly behaviour, proper transmission, style. In this connection men are said to differ from animals in formulating and keeping to rules, in stylish behavior. Transmission of knowledge, of roles is preferably expressed by *kakari*. Here is another example, Hollandia, end of May 1953: our Kamoro 'boy' Josef giving information about the conclusion of his wedding, tells me that while sharing the last meal with his mother, by way of *kakari* she breaks the fire-tong used to handle the layers of the ball of sago for her son. 'Now you move into your wife's and wife's parents' house. She will take over from me [transmission, JP]; she will prepare your sago; my hands are scorched from doing so.'

Jeraya, west of Kaokona, 1 October 1952: I am invited to attend the selection and cutting of a tree in the forest, from which a spirit-pole (*mbi-tòrò*) representing recent dead will be manufactured. This one is meant to be erected in front of the ceremonial house of the 'male' *Kawàre* ritual, the counterpart of the 'female' and equally crucial *Emakamè* ritual. Men-in-the-know go ashore; the uninitiated youngsters are ordered to stay behind in the canoes. I am initially asked not to go ashore but by appealing to my acknowledged participants' status of *peràpoka* = old man, I am at last admitted with a smile to join the men, the *otèmakò* = those entitled (*amakò*) to the secret (*òtò*). Their leader takes me to the selected tree. The men have already cleared the roots. They are busy manufacturing a secret ladder of about 8 metres which is then placed against the tree. The leader climbs it in a ritual dance, showing a dignitary, a young man called David who acts for the first time, how to do the trick. Dressed up in a cassowary frock and plumes the latter then climbs the ladder, followed by his sister's husband, an accomplished dancer. David makes an incision in the tree right under the top with a machete. His brother-in-law does the real work, removes the top and then descends the ladder. David makes himself comfortable sitting on the tree's upper end. He hides behind a camouflage of leaves and twigs. He impersonates a king's parrot (*bòpokò*), after which one of the localised descent groups (*taparu*) has been named. The ladder is removed and destroyed. Its bits and pieces are hidden. The men-in-the-know, divided in two parties tradition-ally denoted as right and left, lie down right and left from the tree. They hide under a cover of leaves and behind a make-shift partition. They behave like dead, tongues protruding, and hold secret tools, to wit digging-sticks, wedges and rattles said to produce the voices of spirits. The uninitiated youngsters are then called to the scene. They are instructed to remove the partition and the leaves: the secrets are revealed and transmitted to the next generation. The human digni-taries of the tree/spirit-pole are said to share their souls with the tree: *ipu enakoa* = soul/spirit one. Then the youngsters are instructed to look upwards. The impersonator of the king's parrot drops his camouflage: another revelation. The initiates wonder how on earth the parrot-man managed to climb the bare tree and perch on the top. The parrot-man slowly and solemnly descends, aided by his brother-in-law and the overawed youngsters. The latter then witness the cere-monial cutting of the tree, blown at with lime powder. The *òtèmakò* lie upon the trunk: they identify with it/him. Their nails rhythmically grate its surface: they caress the body after the painful removal of branches and bark/skin. The rope to drag the trunk to the riverside is produced from a secret spot: another revelation. Also, the roller-chunks of wood to move the tree to the canoe are shown. Pretending that the trunk will be loaded into a canoe, the men remove the canoe at a split moment: the trunk splashes into the water: a case of impres-sion management. All these secrets have been transmitted in a ritual drama. It ends up with massive wailing by the adult men: childhood of the initiates passed away they are adults now. At the performance of a wide array of other rituals by men and – separately – by women, similar and different modes of transmission are practiced with the explicit aim that the grand cycle of rituals which constitute the focus of Kamoro culture, is perpetuated (for a description see Pouwer f.c.).

Kamoro discern a staggering number of *amakò*-positions, of entitle-ments to particular roles, of activities, and of exercising power over a plethora of phenomena. Not only in ceremonies and rituals where even minute activities, such as presenting a ball of sago or hanging pork sides on the wall of a ceremonial house, are exclusively claimed by particular dignitaries, but also in daily life. There at least fifteen *amakò*-positions dealing with the treatment of ailments, such as cold feet, deafness, eyesore, pneumonia, coughing, rheumatism, framboesia, madness and so on. Entitlement to land (*taparè*) is indicated by it: *taperamakò*. Also to sago areas and the handling of sago: *amotèmakò*. There are *amakò*-specialists controlling individual phenomena of nature such as sunlight, heavy rains, winds, thunder, lightning, floods, infertility of sago trees, or women, abundance of fish or the lack of it, and so on. The power ascribed to these persons may be used for the benefit but also to the detriment of women

The term *amakò* is significantly related to the notion of *amòkò* the omni and ever present 'in the beginning'; culture heroes are called *amòkò wé*. In Kamoro cosmology men and the phenomena of nature around them are interconnected: they are of one soul, *ipu enakoa*. The *amakò*-persons transmitting from time immortal, cosmology's 'vertical' dimension so to speak, control and manipulate its 'horizontal' interconnections. Hence the irreversibility of their position. Also, their position cannot be held or acted out by persons who are not entitled to it. I witnessed various occasions in ritual, in the course of which particular parts of it or particular objects were left out because the *amakò*-person concerned was not available. Having others do the job would bring about sickness or death.

When I started fieldwork in New Guinea in the 1950s it was asserted – and I tended to believe it – that its (social) structures were loose, open. What I did find was a *flexible* social structure and *strict* adherence to solemn wording of myths and songs and to rules of rituals and cosmology.

References

Pouwer, J. f.c. *Gender, Social Formation, and the Ritual Cycle in West Papua: A Comparative Analysis of Two South-Coast New-Guinea Cultures: Kamoro - Asmat* Leiden, KITLV Press.

Getting Answers
May Take Some Time...

THE KUGAARUK (PELLY BAY) WORKSHOP ON THE TRANSFER OF
INUIT QAUJIMAJATUQANGIT FROM ELDERS TO YOUTHS,
JUNE 20 - 27, 2004

Cor Remie

When I travelled to the central Canadian arctic in 1973 for my first fieldwork among the Nattilingmiut of Kugaaruk (Pelly Bay), I encountered a community amidst a process of rapid transition. Formerly fully nomadic, the Nattilingmiut had started to congregate around the mission post at the mouth of the Kugaaruk River in the early 1950's, building temporary shacks there. Four years before I arrived, the Nattilingmiut had become fully sedentary. The RC Mission led co-operative had made a bid on a Canadian government contract to build prefab housing and won it. The houses and other building had been put up in the summer of 1969 and when I arrived the community was still busy finding its way of living in a permanent setting. Established in 1935, RC Mission of the Oblate Fathers was still very present in the community, although that situation had started to change too as the government of the Northwest Territories was taking over public services (schooling, healthcare) that had traditionally been provided by the RC Mission.

During that first visit I was highly interested in the question to what extent traditional religious beliefs were still held and practiced. A diary, written between 1958 and 1964 by Bernard Irqugaqtuq at the request of Geert van den Steenhoven, suggested that shamanistic practices were still carried on and basing myself on this information I made an attempt to get some more insight into the matter. It became one of my big frustrations during that first year of fieldwork. Discussing the matter with informants invariably failed: all they wanted to do is show me how good Catholics they had become. Shamanism was something of *taipsomanialuk,* of a long time ago. They would state adamantly that they had broken with that past and that they were now *maliktunik*, followers of the missionaries. In this respect, Bernard was even more tacit than his fellow Nattilingmiut. Given the RC Mission's strong presence in Kugaaruk I had anticipated such behaviour, but I was stubborn enough to believe that with some patience I might be able to break through that icy 'Catholic' surface and catch a glimpse of what was hidden behind. Indeed, I did catch a few glimpses, but not as a result of a deliberate research strategy, but rather by chance as the following example illustrates.

On a chilly morning in August 1974, Bernard Irqugaqtuq (my key informant), Sam Inaksajak (his son-in-law) and made preparations for a hunting trip. Bernard needed some new lines for his dogsled and suggested we go hunting *ugjuk*, bearded seal. An icy wind blew from the North when we set out for Arviligjuaq, Pelly Bay, to go hinting at the other side of the bay at a place where *ugjuk* is usually found. The ride to the other side was rough, because Arviligjuaq is shallow and already a little bit of wind results in disproportionate high waves. Almost soaked to the bone, we arrived at Ungilitaituq at the other side and took temporary refuge ashore in the hope that the wind would soon subside and the waves quiet down. Which they did after half a day. We then started our hunt, but sighted no *ugjuk*. Hours passed and then suddenly we saw one. Bernard managed to drive the mammal into a little cove that was blocked off from the bay by a little island He took his rifle, aimed, pulled the trigger, but nothing happened. Sam then gave it a try, and again nothing happened, the rifle didn't go off. Bernard gesticulated that I should take a shot, and the same thing happened to me. My rifle refused also. With a deep sigh Bernard mumbled '*taamna ugjuk kringaschalukiuq*', that bearded seal must have powerful helping spirits. I asked him to explain what he had just said, but he kept silent. A little later, we had gone ashore, I asked Sam what Bernard had said, but got an evasive answer. When I kept asking, Sam finally pointed at the little island that blocked the cove off from the bay and said: '*tuurngartuujuq suurqaima*', that is *tuurngartuuq*, the place of the spirits, that's why...

It is events like this – and I must admit there were not too many – that made it clear that behind the scenes something was going on that did not exactly express 'good Catholicism'. However, I had to wait thirty years before I could discuss that 'something' quite openly with the same people that so tacitly put up their 'Catholic facade' in 1974. What, then, is the story behind this story?

Between 1974 and 2004 the arctic scene changed dramatically. Increased *qabluna* (White) encroachment on Inuit lands led to counteractions in the mid-1970s which took the form of a land claims movement. During the next two decades, land claims issues and discussions about self-government dominated the northern political debate. In 1996, after twenty years of painstaking negotiations a final agreement on the *Nunavut* (Our Land) land claim could be signed which opened the way to the establishment in 1999 of a new territory, *Nunavut*, that was governed by an Inuit dominated public administration.

From the very beginning, the new Nunavut government made it a point to rewrite the history of the North. Hitherto depicted as passive consumers of culture change, the new ideology now focused on correcting that image. Recording IQ (*Inuit Qaujimajatuqangit*, traditional Inuit knowledge) became an important government program. By recording old wisdom and transferring this knowledge to young Inuit, the Nunavut government hoped to take the edge off some of the most pressing social problems among the young – suicide – by providing them with a new moral framework and value system that could assist them in redefining their identity as Inuit.

In this wider context, I took part in a workshop that was organized the Kugaaruk Elders Society in cooperation with the department of Anthropology of Laval University, Quebec. The project was intended to help youths to re-connect with their culture, and enable Elders to resume their roles in community life through their participation in the transfer process. Frederic Laugrand, Laval University, and Jarich Oosten, Leiden University, who had also facilitated earlier workshops in Rankin Inlet and Arviat, facilitated the workshop. I was invited because of my prior fieldwork in the area. Together with eight elders we developed an agenda of topics to be discussed. Among these was the role Inuit played in the process of Christianization and the way this process had impacted on traditional shamanism. All workshop sessions were recorded on audiotape and videotape and an Inuit interpreter took care of the simultaneous translation.

It is during this workshop that most of the questions that I had raised in 1974 were addressed. Thus Jose Angutingurniq, once a tacit informant, now told in a matter of fact way how shamanism had continued to function since the arrival of the missionaries in Kugaardjuk and still did.

> Before the missionaries came, we had *angatkut* (shamans) who could help us to overcome problems and cure illness. When the missionaries came they brought prayers, but also medicines that helped cure the sick. So do the *qabluna* doctors. But sometimes you have to resort to the old practices. Take for instance the case when you are out hunting inland, four, five days of traveling away from the settlement and you get sick or you have bad luck continuously? What else can you do…?

Jose didn't finish his sentence, but what was implied was clear. Later, during the workshop, Jose led a demonstration of the *qilaniq* (head-lifting), a shamanistic technique to interrogate the helping spirits to find out what the causes of some mishap or illness are.

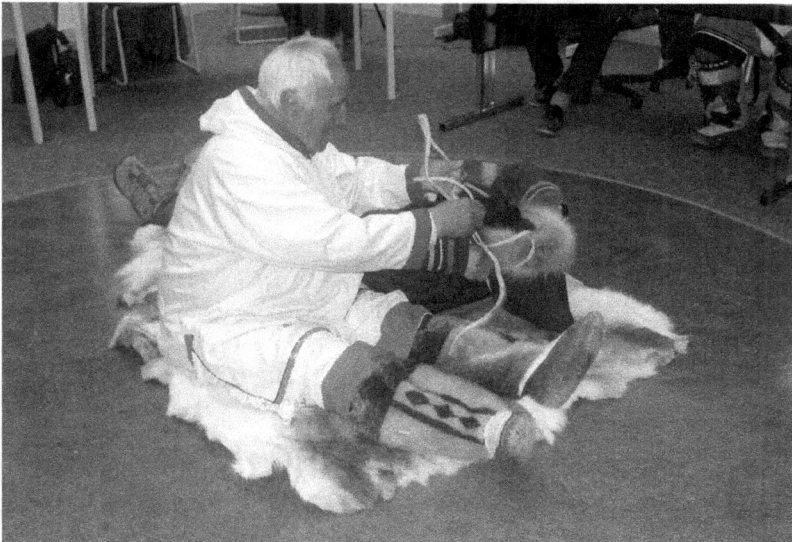

Jose Angutingurniq demonstrating qilaneq. *Photo C. Remie 2004*

The demonstration took place in a very solemn atmosphere and several young people participated. What struck me was the great care that Jose took in showing us the practice. Repeatedly he told us that it was just a demonstration, not the real stuff. But he kept repeating this so many times that one wonders... After all you never know!

In the context of this Liber Amicorum it would lead too far to elaborate on the results of the workshop in minute detail. What the above suggests is that in doing fieldwork there is a specific time for asking questions and for getting answers. In the Kugaaruk case, the demise of the RC Mission's influence over the years and the changing relationship to qablunait (whites) in general certainly played a role. But that doesn't explain it all. During the workshop I also learned that getting answers is a matter of age. When I did my first fieldwork in the Arctic, I was barely thirty years of age, too young to be entrusted with such delicate knowledge. In 2004 I had apparently reached the age for getting answers. Though cultures and circumstances differ, I am convinced that my colleagues must have had similar experiences.

Conflict in the Classroom: Values and Educational Success

Marianne Riphagen

In 2004 I conducted fieldwork in a Central Australian Aboriginal community.[32] The decision to complete my degree in cultural anthropology by means of research in Australia was inspired by the enthusiasm with which Ad Borsboom had always lectured about the Pacific. Under Borsboom's supervision, I examined why the educational results of Indigenous Australian children at 'remote' community schools still fall behind those achieved by their non-Aboriginal peers of the same age. Several studies, carried out by Australian governments and scholars, have concluded that the achievement of equitable and appropriate educational outcomes still has a long way to go (MCEETYA 2001).

Researchers have produced several theories to explain impediments to Aboriginal school success. These theories range from distinctive learning styles (Christie 1986; Hughes 2004) to Aboriginal resistance (Folds 1987). Other scholars have held the supposed supremacy of Western values over values of Indigenous children responsible for Indigenous children's poor performance at school (Hewitson 1982).

This paper considers a different and frequently disregarded dimension of value conflicts in Aboriginal classrooms. Instead of examining the negative influence of Western values underlying the curriculum on Indigenous students, I focus on non-Indigenous teachers' experiences of and responses to value conflicts. I contend that value conflicts affect non-Indigenous teaching staff to such an extent, that their ability to teach is effectively constrained. As a consequence, Indigenous children's school results are negatively influenced.

---

[32] To protect the privacy of staff members and students at the Aboriginal school, I have chosen not to identify the community where I conducted my fieldwork. Similarly, the names of non-Indigenous teachers in the text are all pseudonyms.

Values in the Classroom

The Aboriginal school for primary and secondary education where I conducted my fieldwork between October and December 2004 had fifty-two children enrolled at the time. These students were divided over four classes. Although the school's staff included four Aboriginal Education Assistants and one Aboriginal teacher, non-Indigenous teachers taught the majority of lessons. Before discussing the interaction between Aboriginal and non-Aboriginal values in the school's classrooms, I will define the concept of values. In my thesis[33] I employ Aspin's (2002: 16) definition of values. He states that:

> Values are those ideas, conventions, principles, rules, objects, products, activities, procedures or judgments that people accept, agree to, treasure, cherish, prefer, incline towards, see as important and indeed act upon. Such things they make objects of admiration, high levels of aspiration, standards of judgment, prescriptions for action, norms of conduct or goals of endeavor in their lives and commend them so to others.

Non-Indigenous teachers at the community school frequently display an awareness of the potential influence of their values on the Indigenous children they teach. One of the teachers relates: 'Our values can pose a problem. It's our values that underlie the education of these kids. It is not necessarily something that the kids find important.' However, my research has brought to the fore that students, rather than passive victims of dominant Australian values underlying the curriculum, are active participants in their interaction with Western education. Instead of accepting the existence of Western cultural beliefs, approaches and ideologies in the curriculum and internalizing its content, students of the Aboriginal community school bring their own values into the classrooms and adhere to these.

Autonomy constitutes the most important value articulated by Indigenous students at school. In the Indigenous community where I

---

[33] For an in-depth conceptualization of the concept 'values' I refer to my MA thesis: Riphagen, M. 2005. *My Values, Our School: A Study of the Relation between Interacting Cultural Values and Educational Results at an Australian Aboriginal School on the Pitjantjatjara Lands* Nijmegen, Radboud University, MA thesis.

conducted my fieldwork, parents value and work to develop autonomous characters in their children. This means that children are encouraged to make independent decisions, have the right to choose independent action and enjoy social equality with adults to a great extent. Adults place limited constraints on the behavior of small children and rarely force them to conform to their will (Schwab 1998). As a cultural theme, the core value of autonomy influences several Aboriginal values and beliefs, most importantly those relating to school attendance and communication.

Their autonomy gives children the freedom to decide whether or not they will attend school. This means that students frequently leave the classroom during sessions or after breaks. When children experience feelings of discontent in the classroom, are bored with the lesson, incapable of doing their work or simply feel hungry or tired, they decide to disappear from the class or not to come back after breaks. Indigenous students also independently choose at what time, if at all, they will arrive at school. Often, children turn up at school when classroom sessions have already started. Occasionally they do not attend for several days.

Children attending the community school also express their autonomy in communication with teachers. First of all, they exercise the 'right' not to listen when teachers talk. Secondly, students enjoy the 'right' not to answer questions and to refuse teachers' requests. Harris (in Lipka 1992: 47) argues that children in many Aboriginal societies enjoy the right to speak but not to listen. In the same way it is a privilege and not a right to receive an answer to a question. Harris (1988: 74) has also identified different attitudes towards questions. Many Aboriginal people, he claims, consider the act of posing numerous questions as an invasion of their privacy. To ignore questions in the appropriate contexts is regarded as a right and not interpreted as rude. At school, students can be observed articulating their autonomy when they ignore teachers' questions, disobey requests or talk as instructions are given. Children frequently do not respond, or only after several warnings, to demands they consider a violation of their right to independence.

The value of autonomy conflicts considerably with values adhered to by non-Indigenous staff. For instance, non-Indigenous teachers emphasize the value of education. As part of that, they identify school attendance and achieving the highest possible results as crucial. These values become explicit during interviews and in those instances when teachers follow children who run away from the classroom to convince them to attend lessons. Classroom routines also underline the value ascribed to attendance. For example, Julia always marks the names of those children attending her classes on a large whiteboard in front of the room. Thus, Julia confronts her students, who are intrigued by the marks behind their names, with the value attached to their presence.

Teachers similarly emphasize the value of respect. They interpret respect as students listening to teachers, obeying requests and acknowledging the authority of adults. Non-Indigenous educators at the community school have been trained at university to educate children who, for the most part, answer and listen to their teacher when required. Samuel explicates the value ascribed to listening when he states:

> It seems to me that local Indigenous people in educating their children generally don't demand engagement. We do. I am a teacher and I am here to teach. While I am teaching I expect everyone to listen to me and to be engaged.

Value Conflicts and Performance

The ways in which Indigenous students at the community school articulate their autonomy conflicts with values adhered to by non-Indigenous teachers. These value conflicts seriously influence teachers' state of mind, beliefs and well-being. Consider for instance the following statement by Maddie:

> It is so different here. The kids have the power. They walk out of the classroom when they feel like it. They run if they want to run. Do whatever they are interested in. That has been a big challenge for me [...] Here the kids decide for themselves. They don't do it if they don't want to. It is completely dominated by the kids.

The teacher goes on to say: 'I put so much energy in just functioning

[...] I feel really spent now [...] I went with feeling comfortable in the classroom to not feeling comfortable at all.'

Curriculum modification represents one of the consequences of the influence of value conflicts on teachers (Folds 1984). Teachers construct their own curricula conforming not to criteria implied by educational goals but simply to those criteria demanded by the need to cope. Non-Indigenous teachers at the community school regularly introduce passive learning activities or terminate lessons early. Passive learning activities are those activities like watching animation videos, playing sports, playing games on computers or drawing pictures and coloring in, activities that do not directly contribute to the attainment of literacy and numeracy skills by students in any active way. Often, passive activities like the playing of a game are promised to children on the condition that they complete their work first. But, when children do not wish to engage in learning or decide not to listen to the teachers, teachers terminate lessons or use games to solve conflicts. Teacher Ellen explains:

teaching in mainstream I would never use videos in the classroom, because I consider these as a form of enjoyment [...] Here I use videos with the children just to keep me sane, as a form of maintaining my sanity. Also, watching a video with them enables me to contain their behavior.

It seems reasonable to contend that this frequent drawing on passive work and the early termination of literacy or numeracy lessons negatively influences Indigenous students' measurable school results. As teachers feel compelled to teach less literacy and numeracy, the two important skills on which children are being nationally assessed; children's results will most likely be less satisfying. Teachers realize that students, for whom English is their second language, need to be exposed to many hours of intensive language learning as well as to mathematical tasks in order to gain important skills. However, value conflicts obstruct the teaching of a satisfying amount of literacy and numeracy lessons.

In conclusion, it can be stated that the relationship between values and Indigenous children's educational results contains a thus far under researched dimension. Most scholars have focused on the impact of conflicting values on Indigenous school children. However, this paper has revealed how non-Indigenous teachers feel seriously affected by value conflicts in their classrooms. Furthermore, it has drawn attention to the significant connection between Indigenous children's poor school results and the ways in which teachers experience value conflicts.

REFERENCES

Aspin, D., J. Chapman and V. Klenowski 2001. 'Changing Cultures and Schools in Australia' eds. J. Cairns and D. Lauten *World Yearbook of Education: Values, Culture and Education* London, Kegan Page: 122-143.

Christie, M. 1986). 'Formal Education and Aboriginal Children' *The Aboriginal Child at School* 2: 40-44.

Folds, R. 1984. 'Curriculum, Culture and Classroom Social Relations in South Australia's North West Aboriginal Schools' Canberra, Australian Institute of Aboriginal and Torres Strait Islander Studies: pMS 4028.

Folds, R. 1987. *Whitefella School: Education and Aboriginal Resistance* Sydney, Allen and Unwin.

Harris, S. and J. Harris 1988. 'Aboriginal Communication Styles, Assessment, and Social Change' ed. G. Davidson *Ethnicity and Cognitive Assessment: Australian Perspectives* Darwin, Darwin Institute of Technology: 71-80.

Hewitson, M. 1982. *The Hidden Curriculum* Milton, Bayfield Printing.

Hughes, P. and R.J. Andrews 2004. 'Toward a Theoretical Framework for the Development of an Aboriginal Pedagogy' ed. P. Hughes *Aboriginal Ways of Learning* Adelaide, Flinders Press: 208-249.

Lipka, J. 1992. 'Classroom Conditions Which Enhance Students Discourse among Traditionally-Oriented Aboriginal Primary Schools' *Kaurna Higher Education Journal* 2: 46-66.

Ministerial Council on Education, Employment, Training and Youth Affairs. 2001. *Effective Learning Issues for Indigenous Children Aged 0 to 8 Years* Retrieved February 22, 2004, from the World Wide Web: http://www.curriculum.edu.au/mceetya.

Schwab, R.G. 1995. *Twenty Years of Policy Recommendations for Indigenous Education: Overview and Research Implications* Canberra, Centre for Aboriginal Economic Policy Research.

The Teachings of Tokunupei

Gunter Senft

In February 1983 the most popular song of the adolescents of Tauwema[34] was *'Imdeduya'*. It is a rather schmaltzy song with four stanzas, a refrain, a lovely melody, and the following lyrics:

1.)
When the moon rises from the east
I had a dream of you my love:
Labi gibobwaili,   I spoke words of love
Please remember me!
Take me down to Vau,
let me travel along the coast,
come along with me tonight
before you change your mind.

Refrain (repeated after every stanza)

Imdeduyo, Imdeduyo,	Imdeduyo, Imdeduyo,
kwanvedi, bakenu.	move a bit, I will lie down.
Yegu Yolina.	I am Yolina.
Levavegu kesa'i,	They hit me the waves,
nemtamata vovogu.	tiredness (is in my) body
Imdeduyo, Imdeduyo,	Imdeduyo, Imdeduyo,
kwanvedi, bakenu.	move a bit, I will lie down.

2.)

Kalasila isalili -	The sun goes down -
niva'ila wa idamu	calm sea only smooth sea.
Ikeboku ula simla -	It is calm (not windy) my island -

---

[34] Tauwema is a village on Kaile'una Island; it has been my place of residence on the Trobriand Islands for 25 years now. I would like to express my great gratitude to the people of the Trobriand Islands, especially to the inhabitants of Tauwema; I thank them for their hospitality, friendship, and patient cooperation.

deli wala kayoyugu.	with (me there's) only my sorrow.

3.)

Tubukona iyuvola	The moon rises
mapilana obomatu -	at this side of the east -
madagila visigala -	very nice it shines -
iomau ninamaisi.	it is sad for their minds.

4.)

Yum yam, wiki wiki,	Day (after) day, week (after) week,
tubukona - taitu taitu.	month - year (after) year.
Akayoyu ulo valu -	I fly to my village -
avaituta bagisi?	when will I see you (again)?

I liked the song, transcribed it, and sang it accompanying myself with my accordion.

The people of Tauwema enjoyed my playing their song, and one evening after I had finished my 'performance', Gerubara, one of chief Kilagola's sons, came to me and told me a 20 minute long version of the story of Imdeduya and Yolina. Thus I learned that the lyrics of the song which was classified as a '*wosi tauwau topaisewa*' – a 'song about migrant workers (from the Trobriands)' refers with the protagonists' names and in its refrain to one of the most important myths of the Trobriand Islands. In the song Yolina has turned into a worker who lives far away from the Trobriands in another part of Papua New Guinea but hopes to fly back one day to see his sweetheart Imdeduya again. In the myth, however, Imdeduya is a beautiful girl who later turns into the moon; Yolina is a handsome young man who later turns into the sun. All singers of the song did not know this myth any more. I was fascinated by Gerubara's narration and immediately started to transcribe and translate it.

Word spread around that I was working on these data with much enthusiasm, and a few days later, just after I had finished the transcription and the glossing of the myth, Gerubara's mother Sipwesa came to our house and introduced her younger brother Mokopei to me and my wife. Mokopei, a man in his late fifties who lived in Kaduwaga, a neighboring village, asked me whether I would like to hear the real Imdeduya myth, politely hinting that the version of the myth Gerubara told me was far from representing the text of the myth in full. I was more than eager to document his version of 'Imdeduya'. Because he had announced that his narration would be longer than the one of his nephew I prepared two recorders for tape-recording his narration without any interruption. At that time I had learned that the Trobriand Islanders remember long texts as one piece of 'chunk', so to speak; interruptions had the potential to endanger the continuation of the narration of texts recited from memory. When he realized that I was ready for recording he started his narration and finished it after about 90 minutes. His recitation of the myth was very lively and interspersed with the recurrent singing of a slightly elaborated version of the lines that constitute the refrain of the schmaltzy song of our village band, and of a number of stanzas of a '*wosi milamala*' – a harvest festival song. When he had finished his narration a big crowd had gathered around our house. All the people, young and old, had as enchantedly listened to Mokopei as we had.[35] He asked for some tobacco which I gave him with sincere thanks for his great gift for us and my research. As soon as Mokopei had left Tauwema, I started transcribing the tapes.

The myth describes the journey of Yolina who paddles through the Trobriand archipelago in search of Imdeduya. He had heard of her extraordinary beauty and wants to find and marry her. Wherever he lands and goes ashore the chief of the respective village organizes a big feast and offers him his daughter for marriage. He declines all these offers continuing his journey until he reaches the village where Imdeduya lives. After some complications and with the help of some magic he finally manages to marry her and stays with her and her parents in her village. Imdeduya gives birth to a boy and a girl. After some time Yolina and Imdeduya quarrel about their children. Yolina decides to leave her. One night he takes his magic canoe and starts paddling home to his village. Imdeduya notices him leaving and tries to call him back with a magic spell, but he reacts with countermagic. She climbs up a tree to see him better. When he has vanished at the

---

[35] The houses of the Trobriand Islanders are build out of bush materials. The walls consist of woven palm tree leaves. Therefore it was easy for this crowd of people to overhear Mokopei's narration.

horizon she falls down, breaks her neck and dies. Yolina returns home to his village and stays there.

Gerubara had already told me that after her death Imdeduya metamorphosed into the sun and that Yolina after his death metamorphosed into the moon. When I returned to the Trobriands in 1989 Tokunupei, one of my best consultants in Tauwema, remembered my interest in the myth and provided me with further information which is highly interesting with respect to the Trobriand Islanders' eschatology. Imdeduya and Yolina were actually siblings. They are the ancestor parents of all human beings, and their children went to Kiriwina. Imdeduya's and Yolina's parents are Tudava and his wife Moyetukwa. They had two more children, Topilata and Nabwakesa. These two men became the headmen of the underground villages of the dead on the islands Tuma (Topileta) and Bomatu (Nabwakesa) and the guardians of the entrances to these villages.[36] The four children of Tudava and Moyetukwa brought yams to the Trobriand Islanders; therefore they are also called 'Gulagula' – the basic morpheme of this expression is a classifier that is used to refer to 'heaps of yam' (e.g., 'gulayu tetu' – 'two heaps of yams'). During our discussion of these matters I asked Tokunupei whether he also knew the present day names of the villages or at least their former locations where Yolina went ashore and whether he even knew the names of the chiefs who hosted him during his search for Imdeduya? Tokunupei said yes and told me to write down all the place names and to bring them with me on my next visit to the Trobriands. And indeed, when I returned to the Islands three years later he could answer all my questions; sometimes he could even provide further information on places and protagonists in the myth.

Tokunupei's 'teachings' about Mokopei's recitation of the myth (not to forget Gerubara and the anonymous author of the lyrics of the Imdeduya song who started it all) opened up an important access to Trobriand eschatology. Together with Malinowski's (1916) and Baldwin's (1945) publications the two versions of the Imdeduya myth and the cycles of the 'wosi milamala', the harvest festival songs which I collected and which describe very poetically and quite erotically the

---

[36] For information on Topileta see Malinowski 1916.

'life' of the spirits of the dead in their Tuma Island 'paradise' will allow me to document this by now moribund cultural knowledge of the Trobriand Islanders. This knowledge is inevitably superseded by the Christian understanding of eschatological matters. The documentation of Trobriand concepts of eschatology is one of my future research projects. I hope that its result may serve the basis for teaching future generations of Trobriand Islanders what their great-grandmothers and great-grandfathers and their other ancestors once thought about these last things.

The success of every fieldresearch within the social sciences completely depends on the cooperation of the people whose language, culture, behavior, social organization and cognitive style is the target of the respective research. If the people who host fieldworkers are not willing to teach them the aspects of their life in which the researchers are interested, their fieldresearch will fail. However, once fieldresearchers are accepted by the community, they have the opportunity to experience what Agar (1995: 587) in connection with ethnography has called 'rich points':

> When a rich point occurs, an ethnographer learns that his or her assumptions about how the world works [...] are inadequate to understand something that happened. A gap, a distance between two worlds has just surfaced [...] [and] it is this distance between two worlds of experience that is exactly the problem that ethnographic research is designed to locate and resolve.

How this gap is located and resolved, that this work implies a continuous process of give and take, of mutual learning and teaching between fieldworkers and their hosts and consultants, and that this is one of the reasons why fieldworkers are so enthusiastic about their research – both in the field and at home in their studies – is exemplarily described in Ad Borsboom's (1996) monograph *De clan van de Wilde Honing*. We all can but hope that we may be able, or have been able, to give at least a tiny equivalent of that back to our consultants what they gave us with respect to our interests, our careers, and our lifes.

REFERENCES

Agar, M. 1995. 'Ethnography' eds. J. Verschueren, J.-O. Östman and J. Blommaert *Handbook of Pragmatics: Manual* Amsterdam, John Benjamins: 583-590.

Baldwin, B. 1945. 'Usituma! A Song of Heaven' *Oceania* 15: 201-238.

Borsboom, A. 1996. *De clan van de Wilde Honing: Spirituele rijkdom van de Aborigines* Haarlem, Becht.

Malinowski, B. 1916. 'Baloma: the Spirits of the Dead in the Trobriand Islands' *Journal of the Royal Anthropological Institute of Great Britain and Ireland* 46: 353-430.

Consulting the Old Lady

Marijke Steegstra

Older women, 'old ladies', hold a special position in Ghana, particularly in the context of the family. One of those old ladies was my 'grandmother' Lako Sakité, who recently passed away (in July 2007) and who I knew since 1994. She lovingly called me 'my daughter' (*i bi*), and I respectfully addressed her as 'maa' (mother). She was probably born before or around 1915 (nobody knows for sure), and a granddaughter of the illustrious Krobo chief Nene Sakite I (1892†). I was told that her funeral was grand, as befitting an old lady of her status and age. Many chiefs and queen-mothers, and members of the large extended family were among the mourners, who must have numbered up to hundreds of people. A few women from her extended family had dressed up like girls who are being initiated, to portray the work the old lady used to do. She was not only the senior woman in her family and therefore often consulted in family matters, she was also a priestess attached to the paramount chief's 'stool' and a *dipo* priestess, whose task was to supervise girls' initiation rites.

When people say in a ceremonial context that 'we are going to see the old lady', it means they are going to consult the gods or the ancestors. In the Krobo context, the proverbial 'old lady' originally referred to the deity Nana Klowɛki as the prototype of a wise old woman. In the surrounding Akan societies in southern Ghana the same expression is used, but, according to Boaten (1992: 90), the concept of 'consulting the old lady' evolved from an Akan cosmogony, in which women were said to be the founders of the various clans. They were likewise seen as repositories of knowledge and wisdom, therefore complicated issues were referred to them for advice.

Old ladies in general, and particularly first born women, are considered to be ritual experts and as such they play an important part in life cycle rituals and thus in constituting and gendering a person. Lako Sakite used to bath new born babies, and perform some particular rituals in the so-called 'outdooring' ceremony. One such time I watched her bathing a little baby girl and telling her what people do in this world and who she is. She told the baby that she has a father and a mother and how to address them. By telling her that you say 'father' before you say 'mother', she referred to the social importance of the father for his children and of the patrilineal family. She also informed her that she is part of her patri-clan. She told the baby that as a woman she should fetch water, and take care of her body. Later, during the name giving ceremony of the baby, she tied the typical raffia string with white, black and blue beads around the child's wrist whilst showing it its name.

As a priestess, maa Lako also guided many generations of young girls into womanhood and made them 'real Krobo' by performing the initiation rites called *dipo* for them. Despite the great importance attributed to a boy's circumcision when he is one week old, there are no rituals involved. Girls' initiation rites are rather seen as a central marker of Krobo identity and are quite elaborate. Few Krobo women in the area can actually say that they have not passed through the rites in some form. With the help of other priestesses and older female relatives, maa Lako would perform the rites for a few groups of girls in her house every year around April. Each group's initiation would usually take about ten days. The ceremony involves purification rites through bathing with special leaves, sprinkling of a goat's blood on the girls' feet and the use of white clay, but also singing and dancing, testing girls' virginity, and dressing up. If a first pregnancy occurs before *dipo*, the girl is deemed to be socially undesirable and an unfit marriage partner. Although Lako Sakite emphasized that the *dipo* rites were *kusumi*, custom, and had 'always been performed this way', she would not hesitate to send a girl about whose condition she was suspicious to a maternity clinic to have her tested for pregnancy.

Girls who have not been initiated do not marry within the community, unless a man comes from one of those stout Presbyterian families who were among the first converted people in the time of the Basel missionaries (1857-1917). The Basel Mission strongly emphasized the need to abandon the old, 'heathen customs', and even a physical separation from the 'heathen' family in order to be able to become a Christian. Christian churches still do not approve of the traditional rites of passage, *dipo* in particular, and therefore many parents, most of whom are Christians, have them initiated at a young

146

age with the intention of baptizing them afterwards. The nowadays very popular charismatic churches also reject these 'traditional' rites which they reject as 'pagan'. *Dipo* performances and other rites of passage evoke a constant debate between Christian churches and doctrine and local cultural practices. Some Christian parents would therefore secretly send their daughters to maa Lako's house to be initiated, without appearing in this 'fetish woman's house' themselves.

Next to the performance of ritual acts, the *dipo* rites also involve a playfully testing of the girls' skills in household tasks and dancing. Maa Lako knew many of the accompanying songs for the latter. These songs are often proverbial in character and considered part of Krobo cultural heritage. One song she sang, for example, goes like this: 'My father nursed and guarded me to this matured age and so I look plump and attractive'. Every Krobo woman is supposed to know how to dance. The particular dance consists of very graceful hand movements. The rest of the body is held rather tight. The women shuffle forwards and backwards by just moving their toes, swaying their head elegantly to the rhythm of the music. The particular songs are also sung during weddings and other joyful occasions. They create an atmosphere of ancient tradition, but also are a source for entertainment. Especially during the 'outdooring', the coming out stage in *dipo*, the singing and dancing would reach a climax with the girls beautifully dressed with Dutch wax cloths or *kente* cloth and tons of glass beads of great value. Beads are to the Krobo what gold is to the Ashanti. They are worn at every ceremonial occasion and by chiefs and queen-mothers. Maa Lako knew the name and value of every bead and had a large collection of old, precious beads. People often came to borrow beads from her, sometimes for a small fee.

Because of the work she was doing, some people in the area, even some of her own relatives, had been calling the old priestess a witch. After having served the gods as a traditional priestess her whole long life, Lako Sakite was finally baptized in the Roman Catholic Church in 2002, on, what her relatives then thought to be, her deathbed. It turned out to be a well-deserved retirement from her demanding tasks for the last five years of her life. Such an eleventh hour baptism is not uncommon in a country where Christianity is now the dominant religion. Some authors (De Witte 2001; Gilbert 1988: 139) have suggested that a Christian burial, which is much more prestigious, is such a major concern for many Ghanaians, that it is one reason for conversion to Christianity. I am not sure whether Lako Sakite was much concerned about a high-status funeral, but her family definitely was. She probably compromised for the family's sake. The many chiefs and queen-mothers, traditional priests and other dignitaries at her funeral nevertheless reflected the respect she had earned during her life. There is no doubt that she obtained a good position among the deceased in the spirit world and has become an ancestor. Her wisdom and knowledge will now be called upon any time anybody goes to 'consult the old lady'.

References

Boaten, N.A.A. 1992. 'The Changing Role of Queenmothers in the Akan Polity' *Research Review* 8, 1-2: 90-100.
De Witte, M. 2001. *Long Live the Dead! Changing Funeral Celebrations in Asante, Ghana* Amsterdam, Aksant Academic Publishers.
Gilbert, M. 1988. 'The Sudden Death of a Millionaire: Conversion and Consensus in a Ghanaian Kingdom' *Africa* 58, 3: 291-314

A Chain of Transitional Rites: Teachings beyond Boundaries

Louise Thoonen

A chain of *rites de passage* in which teaching formed a major connection, is what my professional relationship with Ad Borsboom characterises. The feature of chaos, often vital in the liminal phase of *rites de passage*, was luckily mostly absent. Instead, the chain predominantly glimmered with inspiration, expertise, harmony and cordiality.

Maria Baru.
Photo I. Courtens

The first bead of the chain was strung in the 1980s when I attended Ad's course on anthropology and religion. His impassioned way of teaching on and knowledge of this theme were striking and inspired me to choose religion as a main direction. Years later, the second bead was strung when I became a PhD student of Ad at the Centre for Pacific and Asian Studies. Then, in a very pleasant and professional way, he initiated me into that new stage and taught me during the process of realising my PhD thesis. By the third, we became co-teachers when we jointly taught MA courses on religion and identity in the Pacific. After that, by the fourth bead, our cooperation went beyond the boundary of science when I required a position at the Bureau of the Faculty of Social Sciences. Ad had already been connected to the Faculty and the Bureau for years as a vice-dean, a position he fulfilled in a way that commanded great respect. By his personal expertise as a manager and through the fact that we both had double identities as a scientist and staff-member of the faculty, Ad moderated the transfer into my new status. The fifth bead was strung during the ceremony in which I defended my PhD thesis. So, during a period of 19 years marked by five transitional rites, we were related in a process of shifting existing identities and creating new ones. It was an honour and a privilege to work with Ad through and beyond the boundaries in this chain.

With pleasure, I remember the numerous excited conversations with Ad as a teacher, deriving from the manifold similarities we increasingly discovered between Aboriginal and Papuan religion, especially concerning initiation rites. The close link between teaching and initiation in relation to shifting existing identities and creating new ones beyond boundaries, is in the below part illustrated by selective findings from my PhD thesis (Thoonen 2005). Like my thesis, the essay is composed around an influential female religious leader, Maria Baru.

Teaching and Initiation
Maria Baru was born in 1950, one year after Dutch missionaries had introduced the Roman Catholic Mission in her native area. Schooling formed the major missionary method and Maria attended primary

school at the local mission. She was a talented pupil which made a missionary priest select her for continuing her education at a missionary boarding school elsewhere. At that time, Maria was 11 years old and she longed to follow the Western-style education of the Mission instead of the 'traditional' way of the female initiation ritual *'fenia meroh'*. Her parents, however, insisted that she would join 'traditional' education. Maria ran away, but she was forced to return.

When she was about 15 years old, Maria was initiated collectively with three other novices from her clan. For one year, day after day, Maria and these novices were taught a deluge of ancestral laws by a female cult leader. Through initiation, Maria became a member of diverse social groups. She had turned into an adult clan member and a gendered person in accordance with indigenous standards. The ritual inheritance and inscription of ancestral rules, knowledge, symbols, and protective powers had guided her into the first stage of adulthood, or more specifically womanhood. The change in gender identity was above all established by the ritual inheritance and inscription of ancestral secrets and spiritual powers concerning female fertility, the names of female ancestors, and rules for appropriate female behaviour. The successful completion of the full initiation process meant, further, that Maria, when achieving the status of a full adult woman, could act as a ritual teacher during initiation.

Despite its profound effects, the ritual had not suppressed Maria's wish to escape her tribal life and obtain a Western-style education. Without informing her parents, she followed a priest and left her home settlement. She started to live at a missionary boarding school, together with her fellow-initiates, and moved further into the missionary domain. There, she coped with her initiation-teachings in a highly selective way. She removed the external tokens of initiation wherever possible, and for the greater part did not follow the rules she had learned with some exceptions. This reveals that individuals, from the palette of possibilities they obtain during female initiation, can choose what to employ. In Maria's case, these were only those aspects connected to the particular sphere in which Christianity was considered to be ineffective ('not strong enough') in her local perception: the realm of ancestor spirits.

So, once initiated, Maria obeyed some of the ancestral behavioural rules and knowledge, and incorporated them into her personal life. She submerged most of them, however, when she opted for self-expansion and moved into the missionary sphere to be educated. She felt that, within this Christian context, she was not able to practice the ancestral ways freely. Instead, during the years that followed, she moved further into the Catholic domain and became a devout Christian. Although Maria experienced some discrepancies and tensions between her identities, as related to 'tradition' on the one hand and Christianity on the other, she did not yet consider them as to be discordant. During those years, she entered new life stages when she married and became a mother. Through motherhood she achieved the status of full adulthood.

Whereas Maria had submerged the greater part of the knowledge acquired in *fenia meroh* for some fifteen years after her initiation, all this changed during a personal crisis which was directly linked to aspects of female gender: procreation and motherhood. During this crisis, Maria experienced visions that led her to become the founder and leader of the healing and prayer group called *Kelompok Sabda* (Group of God's Word), which nowadays has members all over the Bird's Head region (see Ien Courtens's essay in volume). Maria herself experienced the visions as an assignment to re-evaluate and, at last, apply ancestral knowledge she had obtained during the *fenia meroh* rite: the visions made her realize that she must not forget what she had learned from her ancestors. The visions also served as a creative, legitimate Christian way to revitalize ancestral custom.

Maria started to reconcile the potentially conflicting identities of Catholicism and 'tradition' once she had experienced these visions. Through reconciling her social identity, as connected to initiation, with her social identity as connected to Christianity, Maria achieved a more coherent self and created new healing rituals in which she fused indigenous and Christian notions and symbols. Further, she created a new form of initiation with which she started to initiate other truly devout Christians. The prayer and healing group gained a central, innovating position within the religious domain and daily life, especially regarding relationships between 'tradition' and Christianity (cf. Courtens 2005).

In the 1990s, Maria united her clan and Christian identities in a more radical way: she went beyond revitalizing selective parts of the *fenia meroh* rite and reinstated the initiation rite in its entirety, albeit in a drastically shortened, selective way and adapted to the new socio-religious circumstances. While she acted as the ritual teacher, she only passed on those elements that she perceived to be the main sources of clan and, to a lesser extent, gender identity: ancestral rules, strengths, and ancestral key symbols. Within the altered context, new social identities were emphasised, articulated amongst other things in terms of contrast to Christianity. The attitude towards Christianity was, however, ambiguous because her Catholic identity as the main ritual teacher and this identity of the initiates were considered crucial. Furthermore, the new initiation ritual was performed in a selective way in the sense that only elements were chosen that were considered acceptable to present-day, 'modern' initiates.

As this case among other things shows, through ritual teachers such as Maria Baru who capitalised on the altering context, the meanings of initiation rites change over time. The role of such teachers is crucial as these rituals serve as vital vehicles for negotiating identities, shifting existing identities, and creating new ones beyond boundaries.

REFERENCES

Courtens, I. 2005. *Restoring the Balance: Performing Healing in West Papua* Nijmegen, Radboud University, PhD thesis.
Thoonen, L. 2005. *The Door to Heaven: Female Initiation, Christianity and Identity in West Papua* Nijmegen, Radboud University, PhD thesis.

'That Tour Guide – Im Gotta Know Everything': Tourism as a Stage for Teaching 'Culture' in Aboriginal Australia

Anke Tonnaer

Since their early encounters with European settlers, Australian Aboriginal people have allegedly been on the brink of extinction. As was popularly assumed, their 'cultures' would not be able to deal with the onset of modernisation that the arrival of the settlers in 1788 had heralded. The trope of culture loss has persisted ever since, and continues to exert its influence into the present. A prominent frame within which a process of 'losing culture' is entertained and through which it may be countered today, can be found in forms of Australian cultural tourism. Invigorating culture in a tourism context ostensibly works to preserve a vital Indigenous 'heritage' as well as to educate younger generations in the value of that 'heritage'. Furthermore, cultural tourism is presented as a key to providing non-Indigenous Australians and overseas visitors with a constructive introduction to the diversity of Indigenous Australian cultures.

Notwithstanding the appropriateness of this faith in certain benevolent effects of tourism as well as in the kind of knowledge that can be disseminated in such settings, the encounter between tourists and Aborigines has emerged as a significant context in which a conception of 'Aboriginal culture' is cultivated and performed in continuous reference to a non-Indigenous presence. Merlan (1989: 106) notes that an emphasis on "culture' objectified as goods, products and performances' has become increasingly prominent, as has the idea that 'culture' 'as a distinctive repertoire... differentiates Aborigines in general from Europeans' (106). The point I wish to develop in this paper follows onto Merlan's observations (1989; see also 1998). Seen from the Indigenous perspective, the presence of tourism, I argue, helps to forge and sustain a sense of identity and to gain recognition as an Aboriginal person in relation to non-Indigenous others in a valuable way. In a time in which much of Indigenous affairs and policy development is discussed negatively in Australia the value of an affirmative interface with non-Indigenous people becomes great. I suggest that the rather trouble-free nature of 'Aboriginal culture' in tourist performances provides an appealing notion, serving as a type of 'antidote' to the far more obstinate non-tourist practice as well as the non-Indigenous scrutiny of the transmission and maintenance of knowledge in, for instance, issues of land rights and Native Title that continue to affect Aboriginal people's lives (cf. Merlan 1998; Povinelli 2002).

'Come Share Our Culture'

The data I present here on the Indigenous tourism enterprise called *Manyallaluk Cultural Tours*, have been derived from fieldwork I conducted in 2004 and 2005. The company is named after the Aboriginal settlement, Manyallaluk, which is situated about 100 kilometres south-east of Katherine in the Northern Territory in Australia. Founded in 1991, and Aboriginal owned since 1993, Manyallaluk attracted about 2500 visitors on average annually, inviting them to 'come share our culture'. The tour that operated in the tourist season of 2004 and 2005 consisted of a one-day interactive experience. It entailed a morning bush walk during which tourists learned about the various uses of different plants and trees, followed by a series of demonstrations and opportunities for tourists to have a try themselves in the afternoon, such as basket weaving, fire lighting, and spear throwing. The vital feature of this tour lay in the possibility to meet and establish an exchange with an Aboriginal person. Manyallaluk abounded, according to persistent tourists' comments, with 'friendly people'.

The positive capacities ascribed to tourism as mentioned above were persistently and actively endorsed by the senior Aboriginal tour guides of the Manyallaluk enterprise. In their views of the process of culture sharing in tourism, I discerned a particular historical image of Aborigines as 'wild people'. I propose here that this remarkable self-presentation points to the possibility that the continuous rhetorical emphasis on an ideology of 'sharing' and 'learning' in their role as tour guide may not have indicated an *actual* process of knowledge conveyance either to tourists or young Aborigines. Rather, it served to conjure up a positive Aboriginal identity in contrast – one that reflected, in adaptation of Ortner's phrasing (1999: 148), a sense of agency of how to acknowledge the overwhelming force upon them to be 'Aboriginal' and to shape it to their purposes.

From 'Mad Men' to 'Friendly People'

At the Manyallaluk settlement tourism was not at all perceived as a Western type of spectacle in which Aboriginal people were coaxed to conform to an imposed 'scripted play' (Abbink 2000: 11). Adam and Timothy[37], two senior male guides at Manyallaluk, evoked in conversation with me the figure of the 'wild blackfella', whilst they reminisced the time of their early childhood, which they largely spent in the region around Manyallaluk. They described to me how they traversed what today is Nitmiluk National Park:

T: 'cause in Nitmiluk we used to go raitap [everywhere][38]
A: yeah camping all around that area
T: just like mad men
A: you know, we used to, specially that aeroplane, we used to lukum [look at], this time when all the new plane to come, we used to hide from plane for that noise, run away, you know run
T: we used to run, run away, straight away
A: yeah you know like a wild people
T: like wild people. Today I can sit down here and toktok [talk], not long time I used to run away.
A: we bin a little wild.

---

[37] To protect the guides' privacy, I have used pseudonyms.

[38] In our conversation the guides spoke partly in Kriol, i.e. a type of Aboriginal English that is recognized as a distinct language. I have, therefore, maintained the Kriol words where these were used.

Morphy and Morphy (1984) have noted that the image of the 'wild blackfella' refers to the Aborigines before colonisation. More specifically, it should be understood not as "an image *from* the past' but as 'an image *of* the past', a justification for the contemporary relationship between Aborigines and white people (Morphy and Morphy 1984: 462; emphasis in original). In accord with Morphy and Morphy's argument, these Manyallaluk guides made a distinction between the quite distant time before tourism and the present time, concurrently the time of their youth and adulthood respectively. They described their former selves as 'mad men' who could be scared by the sound of planes soaring over, and who, moreover, fearfully and shyly avoided any dealings with white people. In reflecting on their historically developed engagement with tourism, contact with white people through tourism became 'both the point of discontinuity between an Aboriginal past and present' as well as 'the context for defining the difference between Aborigines of the past and present' (460). They contrasted the identity of tour guide with the wandering, shy and uncouth 'wild blackfella' of the time before tourism was common practice at Manyallaluk.

Evidently, the rather negative image of 'wild people' is at least partly based on European stereotypes of Aborigines (see, e.g., Venbrux 2001, 2007). As Borsboom (1988) comments, Aborigines have long figured in European social thought as the 'Ignoble Savage'. Yet, I would suggest that these guides at Manyallaluk evoked the image of 'wild people' not to acknowledge the European stereotype, but to assert a positive Indigenous identity instead, and to balance the scales of the power inequity commonly present in encounters with non-Indigenous people.[39] Prior to tourism they felt shame, and hesitated to talk to white people, but increasingly they appreciated that there was no reason to be 'shamed'. In particular, part of their role as tour guides they felt to be to comfort tourists in their encounter with 'Aboriginal people'. As mentioned earlier, a persistent comment by tourists on their experience at Manyallaluk denoted the settlement's 'friendly people'. This kind of sociability was equally mentioned as an

---

[39] See Tonnaer (2002) for a comparable inversion that was put forward by a group of Aboriginal people in their interpretation of an historical event in the contact history with non-Indigenous settlers.

important defining feature of working in tourism by the guides. Their role was, according to Adam and Timothy, to 'welcome' tourists, and to tell them 'don't be shy, feel happy, ask questions'. They had moved away from their former 'mad man's' identity, by intentionally displaying a 'wild blackfella's' antipodal propensities: meeting and greeting strangers.

Moreover, during the day they taught tourists how to act as 'black-fellas'.[40] The guides were proud of their tour, as Adam put it: '"you come all the way to see us", we tell them [tourists], "to learn our culture". So [at] end of the day, some they nearly cry, you know, they don't want to go.' The guides' emphasis on the aspect of learning in their understanding of their input in tourism aligns with an idea of 'civilisation'; tourists were, in effect, being cultured into a 'blackfella' world.

The Tourist Space – An Appealing Stage

Working in cultural tourism required a certain cultural knowledge. Timothy stated: 'because tourists, when they come, they gotta askim [ask] question. And that tour guide, im gotta know everything.' This 'everything' has, however, increasingly gained an objectified, essentialised nature in the shape of 'traditional' activities. While, no doubt, this objectification process harbours a fragility, the guides maintained that the tourist interface served as antidote against culture loss, by promoting 'culture' to both tourists and young Aborigines. As Timothy continued: 'All the elders that bin work from the beginning, we wanna learn them young one now. Doesn't matter they didn't learn when they were little but when they're working on the job. They learn from there.'

This perception appears a long way from the careful incremental knowledge acquisition that Borsboom (1996) amongst others has described. Here I did not, however, set out to scrutinize the accuracy of the benevolent rhetoric that appraises tourism as cross-cultural and intergenerational didactic medium. Rather, I would follow Adams's astute point (1996: 69-70) that 'deconstructing their "essen-

---

[40] I follow the term that the guides generally used to refer to themselves, also in front of tourists.

tialized" identity' so as to reveal the intrinsic non-Indigenous influence, would ultimately disempower the guides.

Manyallaluk was able to emanate a positive image of 'Aboriginal culture' in a relatively straightforward performance through a range of typical activities. After nearly 15 years of experience in tourism, a 'blackfella way' had developed in conjunction with a tourist presence. In the guides' perception, part of this way entailed not only a reversal of their former appearance as 'wild people', but simultaneously also a potent renewal of their contact with non-Indigenous others: in their status as tour guide they felt a strong sense of agency in shaping their interaction with white people. Their 'blackfella way' on the tourist stage had grown intimately linked to a contemporary perception of Indigenous self. Moreover, it could, as an existential reference, counteract to the more convoluted present-day conditions outside of tourism, in which many Aborigines, including the residents of Manyallaluk found themselves, in particular regarding the ongoing presence of white people.

REFERENCES

Abbink, J. 2000. 'Tourism and Its Discontents: Suri-Tourist Encounters in Southern Ethiopia' *Social Anthropology* 8, 1: 1-17.

Adams, V. 1996. *Tigers of the Snow and Other Virtual Sherpas: An Ethnography of Himalayan Encounters* Princeton, Princeton University Press.

Borsboom, A. 1988. 'The Savage in European Social Thought: A Prelude to the Conceptualization of the Divergent Peoples and Cultures of Australia and Oceania' *Bijdragen tot de Taal-, Land- en Volkenkunde* 144, 4: 419-432.

Borsboom, A. 1996. *De clan van de Wilde Honing: Spirituele rijkdom van de Aborigines* Haarlem, Becht.

Merlan, F. 1989. 'The Objectification of "Culture": An Aspect of Current Political Process in Aboriginal Affairs' *Anthropological Forum* 6, 1: 105-116.

Merlan, F. 1998. *Caging the Rainbow: Places, Politics and Aborigines in a North Australian Town* Honolulu, University of Hawai'i Press.

Morphy, H. and F. Morphy. 1984. 'The "Myths" of Ngalakan History: Ideology and Images of the Past in Northern Australia' *Man* 19, 3: 459-478.

Ortner, S. 1999. 'Thick Resistance: Death and the Cultural Construction of Agency in Himalayan Mountaineering' ed. S. Ortner *The Fate of 'Culture': Geertz and Beyond* Berkeley, University of California Press: 136-163.

Povinelli, E. 2002. *The Cunning of Recognition: Indigenous Alterities and the Making of Australian Multiculturalism* Durham, Duke University Press.

Tonnaer, A. 2002. *The Resounding of a Plane Crash: The Aeroplane Dance and Its Implications in the Social Context of Contemporary Aboriginal Life in Borroloola, 2001* Nijmegen, Radboud University, MA thesis.

Venbrux, E. 2001. 'On the Pre-Museum History of Baldwin Spencer's Collection of Tiwi Artefacts' ed. M. Bouquet *Academic Anthropology and the Museum: Back to the Future* New York, Berghahn Books: 55-74.

Venbrux, E. 2007. '"Quite Another World of Aboriginal Life": Indigenous People in an Evolving Museumscape' ed. N. Stanley *The Future of Indigenous Museums: Perspectives from the Southwest Pacific* New York, Berghahn Books: 117-134.

The Old Fashioned Funeral: Transmission of Cultural Knowledge

Eric Venbrux

The sounds of a *pukamani* came from the bushes near the beach of Pirlangimpi. Accidentally, I had stumbled on a ritual in progress. Why were mortuary rites performed at this time and day, I wondered. To the best of my knowledge, no one had died recently. And why had this rather old-fashioned site been chosen? Rites in this Aboriginal township on Melville Island, Australia, tended to be held on the ceremonial grounds close to the living quarters of the elderly. On that late afternoon in 1988, it soon turned out, however, that not a single adult was involved in the dancing and singing that had caught my ear. Approaching the scene, I saw a group of children, wearing skirts and loincloths. They had painted themselves up with yellow ochres and white pipe clay. A nine-year old boy had taken the lead. He uttered the lyrics of a song, initiated the ritual yells, and directed the dancers. The other ones, when not dancing, kept time by beating two sticks together or clapping their hands. Most of the children were between the ages of four and seven. Besides performing dances according to prescribed roles, they wailed at a small grave. Crying in unified fashion, the children concluded the ceremony.

The nine-year old explained to me that they had buried a dog. From what I had seen and heard, the accompanying ritual struck me as rather archaic. It was reminiscent of the footage of Sir Baldwin Spencer's filming of the local mortuary rites on wax cylinders, in 1912, that I had viewed a few months earlier in the Australian Institute of Aboriginal Studies in Canberra. The children's performance of death rites of the past raised questions about the transmission of cultural knowledge. Why did their actions leave such an archaic impression? At the same time it seemed that the dog burial provided the opportunity to mimic the adult-led mortuary rites (*pukamani*) they had frequently witnessed. The young leader of the children's ritual had earned himself a reputation with an innovative dance. Everyone had cheered and clapped excitedly as he performed. Undoubtedly, he would become a master of ceremony one day. Not only did he prove to be an excellent dancer, he was also able to memorize lyrics in the old language used for ritual purposes. He sang in the chorus with old men at occasions when it were predominantly adults who paid their last respect to a deceased person. Was he – while directing the group of children – practicing for a future role? What was actually happening in the bushes near the beach: was the ritual I accidentally witnessed part of the children's play? Were they exploring the intricacies of ritual behaviour?

Most strikingly, these children mastered ritual aspects that by then had long gone out of favour. Likewise, they staged fights with small spears, whereas these weapons had not been actively used by the past few generations of adults. The secluded ritual of the children for the dog hints at the possibility of a distinct intra-generational transmission of cultural knowledge. In contrast to the knowledge transfer from one generation to another, this learning of children from their peers encompasses a much shorter chain of transmission. The very brief time interval simply does not allow distortion by the knowledge being a distant memory or other factors. Consequently, the (embodied) knowledge is passed on in tact, that is, without the variability often produced in conduits from one generation to the next.

The conservativeness of children's culture has drawn the attention of folklorists interested in collecting intangible cultural heritage. Australian Aborigines belong to the oldest living cultures in the world and hence might be reasoned to 'evidently' have strong traditionalist traits, yet the phenomenon is not just one of our antipodes. Sylvia Grider (1981: 162), for instance, remarks that 'there is no need for the folklorist to scour the Outback of Australia in search of aborigines, for all he needs to do is glance into his own apartment complex courtyard or neighbourhood playground to find a cooperative group of informants whose private worlds are dominated by tradition.' Traditional as the dog burial might have been, the imaginative world of play also allowed for experimentation. While practice makes perfect, it was by no means a mere carbon copy imitation of the adults that created the excitement among the children, as their young leader performed his dances. In fact, a premium is put on originality and individual creativity in the Aboriginal mortuary rites on Melville Island. To adjust to new situations innovativeness is valued.

Conservativeness and innovativeness are two sides of the same coin. Children's culture is characterized by both, tradition and renewal. First noticed by folklorist William Newell, this has been coined 'Newell's paradox' (Fine 1980). The children's acquisition of traditional lore and practices enhances their creativity. What is more, from an early age onwards they are encouraged by their care-takers to dance in everyday life, but during serious activities such as actual mortuary rites many a toddler is often also placed centre stage. Learning by doing is something teenagers shy away from. Younger children tend to take delight in a cheering crowd. Amongst them-selves, they practise the traditional ways ceaselessly and uncomplain-ingly, and becoming slightly older and confident in the various roles, they try to get their act together. The inventiveness of the nine-year old, surprising an audience of skilled performers well beyond middle age, indicates that intergenerational transmission does not neces-sarily take place in one direction. Indeed, I later witnessed a number of adults performing his dance!

While directing his younger peers, the budding performer created a following that could appreciate novelty. For the time being, the juniors had to stick to an age-old pattern, but within a few years some of them might emerge as innovative dancers. Playful exploration of what adult performers were doing spurred them on. Hidden remained the relentless hours of practicing of what seemed sponta-neous at the scene. To put one's mark, the aim of any aspiring singer and dancer in this locality, demanded discipline. The initiated, old men seeking to astonish their audience at a forthcoming seasonal ritual, composed new songs that they practiced for months on end in seclusion. The skill of practicing the un-revealed until the point of perfection was probably acquired at a fairly young age. Unfortunately, ethnographic studies to confirm this point are hard to find. As Lawrence Hirschfeld (1999: 5-6) puts it, 'anthropologists do not like to acknowledge what children do best, which is to learn culture.'

Instead of fighting straw men's claims of culture being static and

bounded, a good deal may be gained from studying children's acquisition of culture by direct observation, as that is what anthropologists
do best. The dynamics of intra- and intergenerational transmission
of cultural knowledge, the practicing of old and new, and stealth and
revelation offer a tempting prospect. Of interest will be the studies by
Ad Borsboom (1978) and Annette Hamilton (1981) in central-north
Arnhem Land. Borsboom, in particular, demonstrates how in a so-
called traditionally oriented society a ritual, intended for small children, can be transformed beyond recognition. Furthermore, he points
out the importance of age-grades in the acquisition of cultural
knowledge. Elsewhere, Borsboom (1996) shows that in this respect
children and the anthropologist are in the same boat. Anthropologists have learned a lot from children in other cultural settings, let
alone of their own children and their peers around. Life histories
have gained some popularity in mainstream anthropology. Yet 'the
life history of culture learning' (Aunger 2000) is still in its infancy.
And I do mean this literally, for an improved understanding of
cultural knowledge transmission would start by focusing on that
stage early in life. Children's culture along with children's agency
deserve more attention from anthropologists than it received to date.

Ad Borsboom's research in Arnhem Land virtually amounts to
such a 'life history of culture learning'. The cultural knowledge he
acquired over the years deepened his understanding of age-grading,
a subject he never got tired of teaching. From 1972 onwards, he stub-
bornly concentrated on a single group of Aborigines, called the
Djinang, and saw their children grow up, and subsequently become
parents and some even grandparents themselves. The honour was
bestowed upon him that one of the children of a new generation was
named Ad. Carefully documenting the changes that occurred over
time, Ad Borsboom has observed that novelties and continuities in
children's culture went hand-in-hand. Important in this respect was
his experience with his own children in the field, who fitted in easily
with local Aboriginal children and their play. When visiting the Tiwi
Islands with my children at age eight and ten, I was similarly aston-
ished: my children experienced neither language problems nor any
form of culture shock, but instead just had a great time with the local
children at school, moving around and playing with other children

in the township and going out bush. A closer look at what and how they learned is probably a meaningful addition to explain what the Aboriginal children performing their ritual were doing.

REFERENCES

Aunger, R. 2000. 'The Life History of Culture Learning in a Face-to-Face Society' *Ethos* 28, 3: 445-481.

Borsboom, A. 1978. *Maradjiri: A Modern Ritual Complex in Arnhem Land, North Australia* Nijmegen, Katholieke Universiteit Nijmegen, Ph.D. thesis.

Borsboom, A. 1996. *De clan van de Wilde Honing: Spirituele rijkdom van de Aborigines* Haarlem, Becht.

Fine, G.A. 1980. 'Children and Their Culture: Exploring Newell's Paradox' *Western Folklore* 39, 3: 170-183.

Grider, S.A. 1980. 'The Study of Children's Folklore' *Western Folklore* 39, 3: 159-169.

Hamilton, A. 1981. *Nature and Nurture: Aboriginal Child-Rearing in North-Central Arnhem Land* Canberra, Australian Institute of Aboriginal Studies.

Hirshfeld, L.A. 1999. 'L'enfant terrible: Anthropology and Its Aversion to Children' *Etnofoor* 12, 1: 5-26.

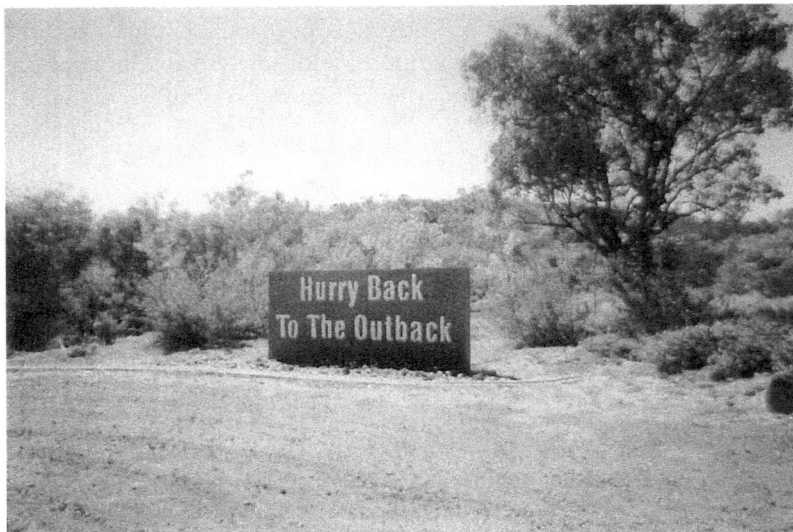

The hurry for the Outback starts now. Photo M. Riphagen

For Product Safety Concerns and Information please contact our EU
representative GPSR@taylorandfrancis.com
Taylor & Francis Verlag GmbH, Kaufingerstraße 24, 80331 München, Germany